# Let's plant & grow together

# Let's plant & grow together

## Your community gardening handbook

**Ben Raskin**

# Contents

# Forewords

The gardening community is a very special group to be part of. Although it looks like a solitary activity, all gardeners are aware they are part of something much bigger, and that the land they work has been cared for by many generations before them and will be handed over to new caretakers in the future. Working at the Royal Botanic Gardens, Kew means that you are part of a wide community of passionate gardeners who are there to support, advise, and listen to your excitement over a new plant. There are also hundreds of volunteers in the horticultural department who make our network even larger.

The term community garden covers an extremely large range of locations and organisations. From large scale market gardens which operate as CSAs (Community Supported Agriculture), to community gardens which act as a base for different local groups to meet and learn a new skill. There are therapeutic gardens where the users often have a specific requirement, possibly even just to sit in a quiet, green space or allotments where many individuals have their own plot of land to tend, coming together for larger jobs and events. Some community garden projects focus on filling abandoned, local spaces with flowers and plants, supported by businesses who see the value in greening a grey space.

Other projects may be built from the demand for locally sourced food, especially with the trend towards lower air miles and improved sustainability. Whatever the project, gardening has always brought people together, to share skills and cake.

Within the walls of Kew Gardens we house a community space, tucked away by Lion Gate. Not open to the public on a regular basis, this space has two growing sites. One half is the staff allotments, where those working at Kew can have a small piece of land to tend, often during their lunch break or after work. The other half of the site is home to our community allotment, a space managed by one member of staff who engages with local charities and community groups to work the plot and learn new skills from Kew's horticulturists, local community gardeners and artists. The community allotment also has its own band of volunteers who show how proud they are to cultivate a part of Kew. This safe space is a productive and cheerful part of the site, giving people who would not normally have access to a botanic garden, the opportunity to be involved and share their wealth of experience and knowledge.

**Hélèna Dove**
HEAD OF THE KITCHEN GARDEN
ROYAL BOTANIC GARDENS, KEW

"Gardening is the most therapeutic and defiant act you can do, especially in the inner city. Plus, you get strawberries."
– Ron Finley

We live in one of the most complex and precarious moments in human history. Environmental and social emergencies abound, presenting an imperative to act. But these crises often feel abstract and impossibly complex. As we listlessly scrub out Marmite pots and darn sock-holes, it's easy to feel impotent, as though we can at best limit our negative impact, but lack the power to push the world toward a brighter future.

Hope comes, not on wings, but from the soil. Shockingly simple and universally accessible, growing a community garden is hands-on, feel-good direct action, with results you can not only see and feel, but also smell and taste.

Community gardens provide food security, boost biodiversity, reduce air pollution, mitigate heat waves, create mood-boosting beauty, break down social barriers, provide nature-based education, and support people's mental wellbeing – often all at once. In their solace we find two rare and vital gifts: connection to nature and community. In providing these things, community gardens address both the symptoms and the root causes of the multiple crises we face, making them truly radical (from radix, meaning "root") solutions. In creating a community garden, you are peacefully demonstrating the power of people and the power of nature. You are forging a portal to a world in which connection, reciprocity and regenerative practices reign; in which sharing, lending and borrowing have replaced over-consumption; and neighbourhoods are alive with flora and fauna. Beyond such altruistic visions, starting a community garden provides entirely self-serving blessings. My own years of grassroots greening have bestowed joy, belonging and a sense of agency I'd never known possible. I've witnessed countless others receive similar epiphanies: a switch almost audibly clicking as they realise their power to effect meaningful change in the world, through collaborative, collective action.

I hope that all who read this handbook go on to cultivate a thriving community garden. In doing so, you will not only reap its bountiful fruits for yourself, you'll also besowing the seed of a greener, healthier, happier, fairer future for all.

**Ellen Miles**
AUTHOR OF *NATURE IS A HUMAN RIGHT* AND *GET GUERRILLA GARDENING*

@octaviachill

# Author Introduction

Gardening is more than just a functional activity. If human beings needed only nutrition, they wouldn't grow flowers or put benches in their gardens. Gardening nourishes our minds as well as our bodies—it is part physical workout, part therapy and meditation. It also reconnects us with nature and tops up our vitamin D. So while many community gardens are simply a way of combining food production with socializing with your friends, some use the many gifts that gardening offers to help educate, inspire, and heal.

Why does gardening feel so good? It is repetitive but challenging. You can let your mind wander while weeding. You get exercise and fresh air, which is vital for the health of a society leading increasingly sedentary lives. On a social level, gardening can take you away from people if you need peace and quiet. Conversely, many of us are searching for connection within our communities, and, in this case gardening can offer a non–threatening environment in which to find this. Whatever your skill level or social confidence, there is something there for you.

## Connecting with Nature

We all love being amazed by nature's wonders. Outer space, jungles, or deserts may be out of reach for most of us, but gardening gives us the chance to get up close and personal with the natural world. Watching a seed germinate and grow, caring for that plant, and seeing it thrive and eventually produce more seeds is immensely satisfying. After thirty years of growing, I still get that excitement as the first shoots emerge from the soil.

## Benefits of Gardening

The very soil itself is good for you, and science is beginning to provide evidence for what we have known for centuries: that having your hands in the ground improves your mood. Complex interactions between the soil and human microorganisms are still barely recognized, much less understood, but as one volunteer who came to a garden as a release from his stressful job said to me, "I always feel calmer with my fingers in the soil." Aside from all of these wonderful benefits you get from gardening with others, you also get the food, which somehow always tastes better when you've grown it yourself and eaten it with friends.

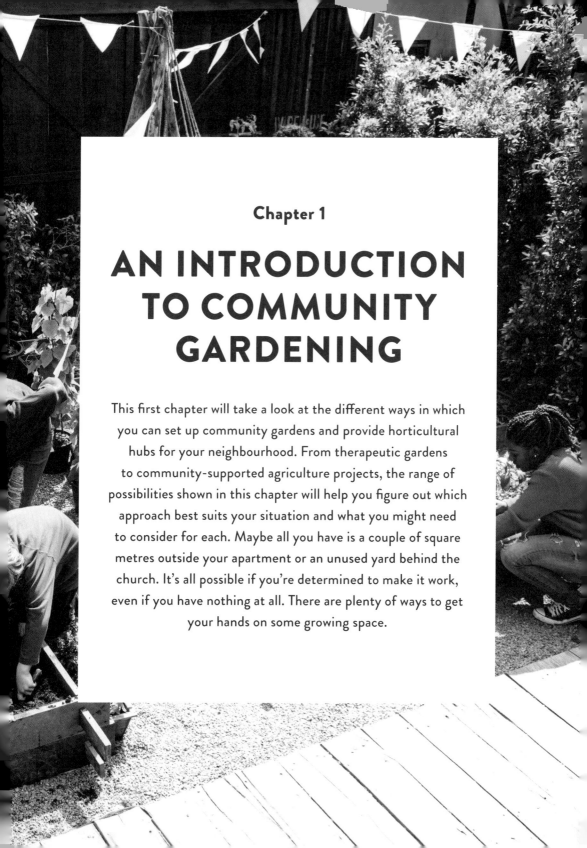

Chapter 1

# AN INTRODUCTION TO COMMUNITY GARDENING

This first chapter will take a look at the different ways in which you can set up community gardens and provide horticultural hubs for your neighbourhood. From therapeutic gardens to community-supported agriculture projects, the range of possibilities shown in this chapter will help you figure out which approach best suits your situation and what you might need to consider for each. Maybe all you have is a couple of square metres outside your apartment or an unused yard behind the church. It's all possible if you're determined to make it work, even if you have nothing at all. There are plenty of ways to get your hands on some growing space.

# An Individual Space for Gardening

For anyone who wants to grow vegetables but doesn't have a garden, the first and most obvious solution might be to look at renting a plot in a public or private shared gardening site. In a city, this might be the only option. Such community sites exist in many places all over the world, and they often go by different names, such as allotments, community gardens, or victory gardens.

Community plots are usually owned by the local government, but trusts or individuals also rent out small parcels of land to private, non-commercial individuals for food growing. My own community garden is owned by a well-known private school, even though the school is located 75 miles (120 km) away from my town.

The sites are often managed by committees, and there will be a set of rules to abide by—for example, to keep the plots tidy and productive. You could lose your plot if you don't weed regularly or mow the grass paths. Sometimes the rules may forbid the planting of fruit trees or the selling of produce grown on the site. Every community garden is different.

**LEFT**
Community plots enable people who don't have access to their own growing space to plant and grow fresh produce and experience the many joys of gardening.

## Advantages and Disadvantages of Renting an Individual Space

### Advantages
› The community is already set up and running—all you need to do is turn up and start gardening.
› You can grow what you like within the rules, and you do not have to take other people's opinions into account.
› You can enjoy the communal aspect without feeling responsible for other people's needs.
› Most sites have water supplies already installed, and you may be allowed to erect a shed or greenhouse.

### Disadvantages
› If you go away for a couple of weeks, you may need to find someone to pick the produce or water the greenhouse plants.
› There may be a waiting list, particularly in an area with a large population.
› The nearest site may be a long way from where you live.

# Adding Value to Individual Spaces

Most people are social creatures, and as much as we love finding some quiet time to meditate among the squash, we also value human interaction. From chatting to a neighbour about growing techniques to asking your garden buddy to give a thirsty plant a drink, unofficial collaboration happens all the time. Working together is cheaper, efficient, and also enhances the experience.

There are many ways to collaborate. Many people join together to share a large delivery of manure or to buy seeds or plants in bulk to get a cheaper deal. More organized groups might even form a club and arrange trips to horticultural gardens or talks from guest speakers. My friend joined forces with five other allotment holders to keep chickens. They each own one chicken, but they keep them all together. This allows plenty of time to go on holiday and weekends away, and only the occasional cleaning out to do, which they share. It has strengthened friendships, and they often now find themselves discussing chicken care and health when they meet up socially.

Occasionally, a forward-thinking municipality or trust takes this idea further by funding ways to add value to community gardening sites. This can really galvanize and support people's natural inclination to collaborate.

**RIGHT**
Getting involved in community gardening is the perfect way to build friendships, enhance social interactions and pass on your gardening knowledge to new gardeners.

# Shared Community Plots

The commitment needed to look after an individual plot on your own is not for everyone. An alternative may be to become part of a larger plan, where the whole community works together and shares the produce instead of each person caring for their own little plot. What can be achieved is something much greater than its constituent parts.

Shared community gardens can be small or big, depending on how large an area you can manage or get your hands on. But larger isn't necessarily better, and there are some great examples of successful community gardens that have sprung up in corners of small towns or churchyards. Particularly small spaces need careful planning, and while their actual produce may be limited, their social output can be huge.

## The Benefits of Collaborating

Community gardens offer a regular and real opportunity for social interaction. I've found that their members have a greater sense of obligation and will almost always make the effort to come and work, even if the weather is miserable.

So much more can be achieved once people start to work together. Days can be organized with a lot of volunteers so that larger jobs, such as potato or squash harvesting, which might take one or two people several days, can be done in practically no time at all. Another benefit is that if someone finds it hard to make a regular commitment, there is usually someone around to cover the core tasks, such as watering or harvesting. That person can then contribute time and effort in return when it suits him or her.

LEFT
Working together and sharing tasks helps to maintain and manage a community garden and allows people to contribute to the cultivation of fresh fruit and vegetables.

# Community Orchards

Orchards are well suited to community growing because they are not particularly demanding on a community's time. The work is sporadic, and the few big jobs that are necessary through the year, such as picking the fruit and pruning, are ideal for work parties. These undertakings are also not too time-critical, making it easy to plan a well-attended weekend work party when members are free.

Planting the orchard in the first place is one such large task that benefits from a community's help, and harvesting, juicing, cider making, and even pruning can also be time-consuming if there are a large number of trees. At other times of year, the work is light—trees don't need watering every day, for example, and, once established, they will cope with weeds. Orchards need their main prune in winter, which is a fantastic excuse to get together in the colder months, and share the work and a slice of cake.

There is another good reason why community orchards are especially popular: they are lovely spaces to be in. They can be used as informal social areas in which kids can play and members can picnic. Some orchards have special areas suitable for gatherings, plays and poetry reading.

People can also develop special relationships with trees, and fruit trees in particular. Planting a tree and watching it grow and start to produce fruit a few years later is immensely rewarding, and blossom time and harvest can even be spiritual.

In southwestern England, there are still many "wassailing" events that take place on Twelfth Night (Epiphany), celebrating the cider apple trees and drinking to their health in the hope of a fruitful harvest for the coming year.

## Practical Considerations

› What fruit to grow? It is especially important to consider pest and disease management requirements, pollination groups, rootstocks and harvesting times. It is always sensible to take advice from an expert, and the nursery who supplies the trees might be the best place to find this wisdom.
› How much fruit will you produce? There will probably be too much to eat, provision may be needed later on to rent, buy, or make some juicing or preserving equipment.
› Is there enough space? Although a massive amount of land is not necessary, growing trees does need more space than vegetables. Even in small spaces, however, you will usually be able to plant a couple of trees.

**RIGHT**
Community orchards can be used for meeting, socialising, and celebrating. They provide a focal point for community activities and increase access to fresh organic fruit.

# Animals in Community Gardens

Animals in a community garden can provide a number of benefits, which include extra produce, weed control, and free manure. You can also upgrade your status to that of "community farm." Bringing livestock into your community growing space is not something to take on lightly, however, so if you want to introduce some animals, here are some of the things to consider.

## What Animals Can Bring

› The most obvious benefit is that animals can provide eggs, milk, and meat, which are all fairly expensive to buy and often tastier when home-produced.
› Maintaining soil fertility is a big issue for gardens, particularly for urban sites that have to buy in compost and manures. Animals help maintain fertility by grazing and returning many of the nutrients back into the soil for subsequent crops.
› Animals can help with weed control. Pigs are great at getting rid of deep-rooting perennial weeds, while chickens like to eat some of the softer leafy weeds.
› Some animals help with pest control. Poultry are particularly good at eating insect pests, and ducks also love slugs.

› Animals eliminate food waste by eating table and cooking scraps, which eases the pressure on landfills while providing nutrition and manure. Choose foods that are both healthy and beneficial for your particular type of animal, and make sure food scraps are managed well so that pests are not encouraged.
› Animals can be great company, making a community space a more attractive place to be. Animals can also help families spend more time at the garden because they provide entertainment for children while the adults take care of the weeding.
› Interaction with and caring for animals can help in the treatment of mental health problems and improve behaviour at school. Sustained contact with animals can increase focused attention in children with attention deficit disorder.

**RIGHT**
Keeping chickens is a great way to use kitchen scraps as feed, making sure that food isn't wasted and being provided with a share of fresh eggs as a result is a bonus.

## Some Pitfalls to Avoid

› Always consult your community before bringing animals into the garden, and be sensitive to vegan and vegetarian members, who may object if the plan is to eat them or their produce. Some people also have allergies to particular animals.

› Keeping animals is very different to growing vegetables and requires a high level of commitment, including financial for feed, vets and possible safe slaughter.

› Someone has to be on site at least twice a day to feed and water the animals. You will also need someone local to the site to be on call in case of escape or illness.

› Fresh and clean potable water is vital, especially for bigger animals, which drink a lot of water.

› Read up on common illnesses and diseases, and make sure you have a veterinarian you can contact if the animals become sick.

› Avoid naming animals intended for the table. Even if you are not a vegetarian, are you really prepared to eat an animal you have reared?

› Animals are happier if they have company of their own kind, so if possible have at least two of any animal.

› Good fencing is essential if you don't want to lose the animals or your plants. Instaling electric fencing with solar panels to keep them charged is a good method.

› Animals also require safe, predator-proof housing. Make sure that animals will be safe at night or when the keepers are not on site.

› Housing must be an appropriate size. Animals will be happier and healthier with shelter from the rain and cold, and shade from the sun. Make sure to provide suitable cover.

# Community-Supported Agriculture

Many community gardens operate perfectly as somewhere for people to enjoy gardening. However, there are ways to expand the model and become more commercial without losing some of the key benefits of community gardening. While some adopt the traditional supply system, where the grower takes all the risk and hopes to make a profit, many have chosen the community-supported agriculture model where the consumer subscribes to the produce via a veg box or similar.

At the heart of community-supported agriculture (CSA) is the idea that those producing the food and those eating it should share the risk and reward. There is usually a full- or part-time grower paid by the members of the CSA.

By making sure of a fair wage for the farmer, the CSA helps to ensure the ongoing supply of produce and the sanity of the grower. This differs from a traditional supply system, which makes money in a good year but loses in a poor one.

## Features of a CSA Farm

In the United Kingdom and United States there is a wide range of organizational structures and distribution models to choose from. CSA farms share some common features:

› There is usually a commitment to an up-front payment and a notice period required for stopping membership.

› Instead of paying by weight or bunch of produce, there is a monthly payment in return for a monthly share of produce. This can mean that there is less to be had in spring, but a glut in the autumn and early winter.
› Some CSA farms require members to do regular work. This need not be field work.
› Most CSA farms hold social and skill-sharing events.
› Some CSA farms choose to eat only what they grow themselves and may take a couple of months off when there is little fresh produce.

CSA farms tend to be larger than purely voluntary community gardens. Paying even a part-time grower will require significant funding from membership income, and enough land will be needed to grow most of the annual vegetable requirements of those members. Many operate successfully on just a couple of acres with thirty or so members.

**RIGHT**
CSA farmers receive a secure income as well as a closer connection with their community.

# What to Do If You Have No Land of Your Own

For many people, particularly those who live in a city, a garden is a distant dream. There are still ways, however, that you can get growing. Even in the most built-up urban environment, there are areas of undervalued grass or scrub that cost the local authorities money to maintain. Over the next few pages, you will examine a range of options for finding a growing space by simply getting permission from the right person.

## Rooftop Gardening

Cities have loads of buildings and, therefore, a lot of shade, so it's not always easy to find ground that gets a decent amount of light. Head upward, however, and you solve that problem. By growing on roofs, you should get full sun for most of the day.

## Planning Your Garden

There are a number of issues to consider if you're planning on creating a rooftop garden.

**WIND** Getting clear of neighbouring buildings helps with access to sunlight, but the higher you get, the more exposed you become. Windbreak materials around the rooftop garden will protect the plants. Most effective will be a semi-permeable structure, such as a trellis or hedge, which will break up the wind and slow it down. A solid fence will cause swirling and potentially damaging gusts as the wind whips up over the top and back down into the garden. Wind can also blow things off a rooftop garden, so it

is especially important to make sure everything is secure and sturdy.

**WATER** For many roof gardens, getting enough water is a serious issue. Sunny, windy spots are liable to dry out more quickly than some sites at ground level. You may be lucky and have good water pressure to allow you to run a hose.

**ACCESS** Getting materials up to and down from a roof garden is a challenge, especially at the set-up phase when containers, soil, and materials for raised beds need to be lifted up. If access allows, consider rigging up a pulley system.

**ROOF STRENGTH AND SAFETY** Unless there has already been a garden on the rooftop in question, it is vital to know whether it is strong enough. Get a structural engineer to look at the roof and tell you what needs to be done. It is also worth getting a railing put up all the way around the garden for safety. In some countries, this may be a legal requirement.

**LEFT**
Urban community gardens can benefit residents with no access to land of their own, creating a space for growing herbs, fruits, flowers, and vegetables.

# Temporary Gardening

Finding permanent space in urban areas to grow plants is difficult, but there are always empty development sites or corners of parks where the landowner may be prepared to accommodate some removable growing containers. Sometimes developers may be prepared to let people onto a site for a year or more if it is sitting vacant for a period of time.

## Portable Gardens

Containers can go almost anywhere and can be of almost any size. With a little ingenuity, it is possible to grow almost anything, including permanent crops such as fruit trees, if the container is large enough. The one downside is that temporary gardens will not be secure. Building schedules and temporary leases can change overnight, so to save having to dismantle your beds every time you have to move on, here are a few ways you can create a portable garden:

**PALLET BEDS** Pallets are designed to be moved by a forklift truck; they are also built to be strong. Making your container garden on a pallet means that if your lease runs out, then you just move it to a new site.

**ONE-TON BAGS** These are the bags that normally contain sand or cement for delivery. Filled to 80 percent with soil mix, they make an ideal container. They take a good depth of soil and the material is woven plastic, so water drains from it. One-ton bags are also strong and have handles at each corner, so they can be lifted by the right machinery if needs be.

**SKIP GARDENS** In some places, such as Kings Cross in London, the idea of portable gardens has been taken to the limits by using large skips to create community gardens. When it's time to move on, the entire skip is simply lifted up and relocated.

**TRAILER GARDENS** Built directly onto a flatbed trailer, these are the ultimate portable gardens. You will need to make sure the trailer can take the weight of soil. Although they are more expensive to build than most other temporary gardens, they are cheaper to move.

## Practical Considerations

While these ideas find a way around the problem of having nowhere permanent to grow vegetables and fruit, there are still a few practical and financial issues that might be a barrier.

› Even large containers will need watering. If there is no tap-water supply, you will need to rig up a water-collection system from nearby local buildings.

› Although ton bags and pallets are usually free, large containers or skips can be pricey; however, they should last for years.

› Unless you have your own forklift or skip carrier, you will have to pay someone to move your portable garden for you when the time comes to change sites.

› Big containers mean a lot of soil. You might be able to source it for nothing, but it is more probable that you will have to pay.

ABOVE
Portable gardens are space-efficient and mobile so they can be moved to different locations.

TEMPORARY GARDENING    27

# Guerrilla Gardening

Guerilla gardeners sow or plant up neglected or wasted space with the aim of improving the environment and cheering up their neighbourhood. Although traditionally done without land owners permission, a much more fruitful relationship can be formed by chatting to the owners who will probably be glad to have green fingers helping them out.

Entry-level guerrilla gardeners could broadcast some easy-to-germinate seeds of ornamental annual plants. You may also need to bring along a bag of compost if the ground is poor.

Choose plants that are tough and easy, because there will be little opportunity to give them care and attention. If you have more time and inclination, try planting vegetables, perennial flowers, or even fruit trees. You could combine the idea of temporary gardening (see pages 26-27) with guerrilla gardening and put your flowerpots or movable gardens in an unused space.

## Guerrilla Gardening Sites

**SMALL AREAS OF GRASS UNDER SIGNPOSTS OR ON CORNERS**
City authorities might be pleased not to have to look after these areas, which can cost money to maintain. Make sure the plants will not obscure signs.

**FRONT YARDS OF PUBLICLY OWNED BUILDINGS** In many cases, budget cuts mean that there are not any funds to do anything with small green areas, for example, around local government offices. Bringing the community in to make use of them can help, but in these instances, the owners may help with the costs of the soil and seeds.

## Practical Considerations

Here are a few simple rules to follow to make sure that a guerrilla gardening project brings pleasure instead of aggravation to the community:

› Choose non-invasive plants that won't spread to other cultivated areas.
› Always leave the area in a better state than you found it. Few people will object if a litter-strewn muddy patch of grass becomes a cared-for bed of flowers or vegetables.
› Return to do some maintenance, even if this is just an occasional check and weed.

LEFT
Guerrilla gardeners reclaim neglected public spaces by transforming them into beautiful green areas for everyone to enjoy.

# Community Networks

In many towns around the world, groups have been formed that are part of larger community networks. The Transition Town model rebuilds community resilience and reduces $CO_2$ emissions, with well over a thousand registered transition initiatives. The Incredible Edible Network emphasizes working together to grow produce, provide training, and support local commerce.

## Transition Network

Created with the mission to create an "energy descent plan," groups within the community looking at transport, energy, education, waste, recycling, and other matters. There is usually a strong food element, not just because it is a vital component of resilience, but because food brings people together.

If there is no pre-existing transition group in your community, then it might be your garden that brings people together and forms the catalyst for a transition initiative. The Transition Network has criteria for becoming an official part of the initiative in order to be sure any group is built on stable foundations, and it coordinates programs across the network, so it is sensible to consider them when planning your community garden. The latest list of criteria can be found at www.transitionnetwork.org. Transition groups offer a supply of people to garden with. Those involved in the transition movement tend to

be already switched on to the issues of local food supply and community. Tapping into an existing group saves time and effort. In return, community gardens can help the Transition Network build momentum.

There will probably be a number of people with the skills and experience that can help community-led enterprises work and survive. There may also be an opportunity to link up with local government.

## Incredible Edible Network

The Transition Network is worldwide but the Incredible Edible Network is only UK based.

The network works with businesses and learning centres and campaigns with others to get people talking and working together about food. Advice on how to join the network and links to umbrella organizations around the world can be found at www.incredibleediblenetwork.org.uk.

RIGHT
The Incredible Edible Network is completely separate from the Transition Network, although the initiatives have a similar ethos, and both seek to strengthen community resilience.

# Children and Community Gardening

Children can get all the benefits that community gardening brings to adults. First, it engages them in growing food. With obesity on the rise among children in developed countries, getting them to eat well can be a challenge. If they've grown the food themselves, however, this is not usually so difficult. Gardening may provide a first opportunity to care for something other than themselves.

An outdoor teaching environment is an area where all children can thrive, including those who may be challenged by a traditional, academic classroom setting. Children may access gardening spaces at their school, on a trip to a large garden or with family at a community space. As well as caring for plants and interacting with people of different ages and backgrounds, a love of plants at a young age may lead to a career in the horticultural industry.

## Practical Considerations

While much of the advice throughout this book applies equally to gardening with young people, there are a few other things to consider when setting up a youth or children's garden:

› Do you have room within your school or youth centre to set up a garden? This may be the simplest way to safeguard children's requirements, but it could be limiting in terms of space.
› Find a partner garden to work with if there is no space within your own setting for a separate garden for children. Keep in mind they may not be geared toward large groups of children. They may need help to build their infrastructure, for example, to include children's bathrooms.
› Do you have staff with gardening knowledge? If not, there will almost certainly be a parent or local resident willing to volunteer.
› Fit the gardening into and around other school activities. Also, plan crops around the school schedule. There is no point growing summer-ripening tomatoes if no one is around to harvest them.
› Some parents don't like their children getting muddy at school, so don't put these kids at a disadvantage. Plant raised beds help keep the children a little cleaner.
› Find someone to care for the garden during school breaks so things do not get out of hand when the children are away.

# Therapeutic Gardening

The benefits of gardening are now being recognized as a powerful tool in recovery, rehabilitation and general wellbeing. Gwenn Fried of the Rusk Rehabilitation program at New York University Langone Medical Centre sums up why the children with autism with whom she works find horticultural therapy so useful: "Nature is non-judgmental, alive, and real. You can touch and feel, plant a seed, and watch it grow."

For a therapeutic community garden, it will be necessary to design both the actual garden and the work plans around the needs of the people using it. Finding the tasks that a specific group of users will benefit from is key, some may benefit from repetitive tasks, while some may enjoy the physical challenge of digging. The success of the garden will depend on finding a team that is able to balance the needs of the garden and its gardeners.

## Health Benefits

In 2014, a UK charity called Target: Wellbeing conducted research that demonstrated the physical and mental health benefits gained from community projects centred around gardening and growing community food. There had been numerous examples of this working in practice, but this study pulled together the evidence. Some of the findings were pretty compelling, to those of us who have witnessed the positive power of community gardening first-hand. The study found that among the participants:

› 92 percent felt more confident to manage their everyday lives.
› 76 percent said that the activity increased their access to healthy food choices.
› 70 percent reported increased levels of physical activity in daily life.
› 67 percent of people reported reduced barriers to exercise or having taken up a new activity.
› 61 percent developed new skills regarding growing or cooking nutritional food.

The results demonstrate clearly that growing plants has a huge potential to change lives. Health professionals will hopefully prescribe gardening and particularly food growing as part of the treatment for many conditions. If working in or creating a garden for users with certain requirements, think about getting training from a charity such as Thrive.

**RIGHT**
Growing your own fruits, vegetables and herbs is not only beneficial to your wellbeing, but it's also a fun activity for the whole family to enjoy.

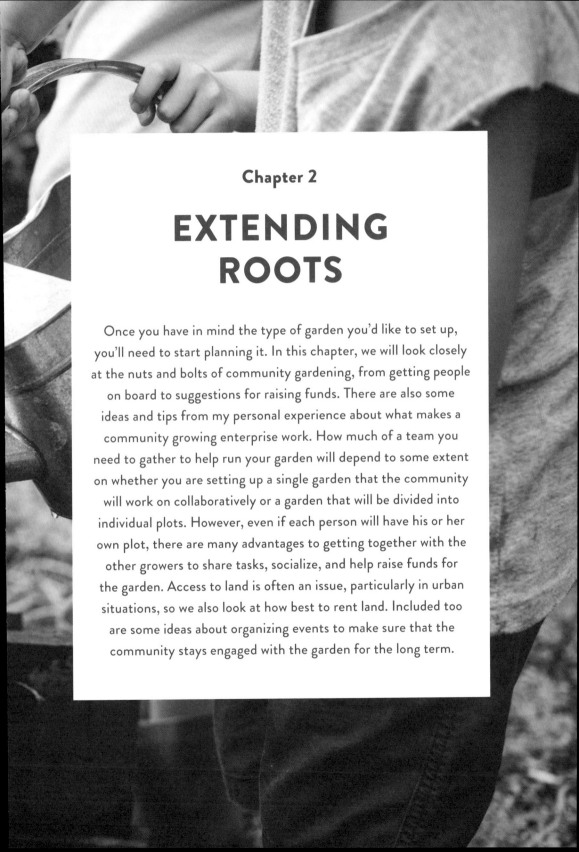

Chapter 2

# EXTENDING ROOTS

Once you have in mind the type of garden you'd like to set up, you'll need to start planning it. In this chapter, we will look closely at the nuts and bolts of community gardening, from getting people on board to suggestions for raising funds. There are also some ideas and tips from my personal experience about what makes a community growing enterprise work. How much of a team you need to gather to help run your garden will depend to some extent on whether you are setting up a single garden that the community will work on collaboratively or a garden that will be divided into individual plots. However, even if each person will have his or her own plot, there are many advantages to getting together with the other growers to share tasks, socialize, and help raise funds for the garden. Access to land is often an issue, particularly in urban situations, so we also look at how best to rent land. Included too are some ideas about organizing events to make sure that the community stays engaged with the garden for the long term.

# From Vision to Reality

To make any project a reality, you need an initial vision and the drive to make it happen. This usually comes from one or two people, and because you are reading this book, this person is probably you. Starting this journey may be daunting, but don't worry. The power of the community can make it happen, and this is why we've put this chapter before the chapter on planning the garden.

Your initial vision may be hazy, perhaps a general idea that you'd like a community growing space, or a dream of sitting with members of your community, eating the fresh produce of the plants and trees you have nurtured. You may never have created a garden before, installed an irrigation system, run a community group, rented land, written a funding bid, or dealt with city planners. Where do you begin? As with any community enterprise, it starts with the community.

## Building the Team

The first step is to gather together a few individuals—a "steering group"—who will develop the "full vision." This does not mean that every detail of a final plan has to be in place at this stage, but if you are going to be able to persuade the wider community and contributors that you deserve support, you need to be able to communicate a coherent vision. If your community garden is not run by the local administration or other paid group, you may need to have a small voluntary team that organizes the distribution of the plots, collects fees, and makes sure that everyone follows the rules.

## Creating the Vision

Use the steering group to create your vision. If you are looking at just a small project with a small number of people, this does not have to be a big piece of work, but it helps to think through some of the challenges, costs, and tasks at an early stage. For larger projects, include your aims, motivations, and potential beneficiaries; if you are looking to raise significant funds, a business plan is essential. Whether you are asking people to donate time or money, or borrowing from them with a repayment program, they will want to know that their contribution will be well used and lead to lasting change.

RIGHT
The size of your community garden will affect how much planning you need to do up front and how long it will take to become reality. However, once spring arrives and work starts on preparing the ground, all the preplanning will be worth the effort.

## Public Meeting

Although it is not essential for all gardens, holding a public meeting can be a great way of getting the community on board, even if they do not want to be directly involved in the project. You can explain at the meeting what your vision for the garden is and what you intend to do to set it up, and this will hopefully garner support and additional members. It may also bring out people from your community that you have never met before, who have the time, skills, and enthusiasm to help your project get off the ground.

## Raising Funds

How are you going to fund your garden? Unless you have a stack of money burning a hole in your pocket, the chances are that you will need to raise money. This might be just a relatively small amount for seeds, tools, and some materials to make soil mix containers. Alternatively, you may be looking to employ gardeners, volunteer managers, and community liaison workers on an ongoing basis. If your garden is divided up into individual plots, the gardeners will mostly take responsibility for their own costs, though there may still be some jobs, like keeping perimeter fencing in good condition, that will need to be funded. You will almost certainly need a formal and legally binding structure if you start to raise money (see pages 46-47).

## Reality

On the pages that follow, more detail is given to the foregoing points so that you can truly bring your vision to reality. Build the team and get some funding, and then you can get started on the really hard work: building the garden and growing some plants.

# How to Run a Public Meeting

Community gardens work best when they have the support and engagement of the wider community, and they also thrive on transparency and communication. For these reasons, at some point during the development of your community garden, you will probably want to hold a public meeting. For the best results, make sure it has clear objectives and a good agenda.

## How to Create Interest

This will probably be your first marketing opportunity, and you want people to go away thinking, "Wow, that's a great idea; I want to be part of it." So, don't make the meeting too long, and try to make it fun. Get a key community character, local celebrity, or local politician to come to the meeting and give the project some support. It will help attract people to the meeting, and while they are there, make sure you have some supporters of the project who will be happy to be vocal about it. People are always more convinced if there isn't just one person endorsing a project.

## Attracting Supporters

No doubt you will be trying to recruit people—for instance, to rent plots or help with running the project. Even if you are only at the early stages, make sure you collect people's contact details and make note of the skills they can offer. This will also help to produce both "evidence of need" and proof of community support to contributors if it becomes necessary later on. Furthermore, if you are looking for financial backing, this is a good time to get that idea out there.

Finally, use the meeting to listen. However good your ideas and plans might be, you will not have thought of everything or considered everyone's point of view. Accept that you may have to adjust your plans.

## Anything Contentious?

Be prepared for the awkward questions. Is there a reason why anyone would be against your garden plans? Do people walk their dogs on the site, or is there worry about loss of wildlife habitat, increased traffic, or loss of privacy? Will the local authorities have any objections? Whatever your endeavour, you will need your community on board.

## Follow-Up

Capturing enthusiasm from that first meeting and channelling it is vital. There may also be an element of confusion if new people join the project with fresh but potentially contradictory ideas. Organize a meeting with your steering group within a week or two of the public meeting while the ideas and buzz are still fresh.

## A Suggestion for the Meeting Format

› Introduction and welcome.
› Outline of the garden project, with a little history; promote the benefits.
› Description of what the garden will offer to volunteers, the community, and other groups that will use it.
› A guest speaker from a similar project elsewhere to showcase what is possible.
› Questions and discussion.
› Schedule a date for the next meeting.
› Offer refreshments at the end to give people a chance to talk about the idea and make connections.

It may be possible to introduce a brainstorming session, splitting the meeting into small groups of perhaps four to eight people. Not only will it bring up new ideas and possibilities, it gives those who are uncomfortable speaking in front of a large group of people the chance to contribute. Ask them to write down their ideas on paper tablecloths or big sheets of paper placed on individual tables.

**LEFT**
Allow time after the meeting so that people can mingle and discuss the project. It will also be a great opportunity to connect with other locals.

# Building the Team and Sharing the Workload

You might have countless skills, boundless energy, a long list of contacts, and no need for sleep, but to make most projects work, a team is necessary. Build that team as soon as possible to give yourself the best chance of success. Cast your net wide for your initial project group and then try to identify people with the skills and approach needed to make your project work.

## Finding the Right People

A common problem is finding people with all the skills and experience you need from within your network or locality. The first step toward overcoming this is to seek out similar projects, meet and talk to the organizers, and use them as good examples of what has worked. Ask for their advice and if you can share their contacts—after all, life is too short to reinvent the wheel. Even if these people cannot get directly involved in your project, they might be willing to help mentor and guide from a distance.

If you need it, get some expert advice, particularly in areas such as soil and garden management, legal structures, business planning, and accounting. There may be public funds available, or you might need to dip into your own reserves. Although it might seem like an extravagance, getting the right advice can save money down the line or even make the difference between success and failure.

For communally run gardens, a steering group can be a good starting point. For instance, when I helped set up a community farm, we had in our group, among others, a farmer, a teacher, a health professional, a food retailer, a lawyer, and an experienced community facilitator, and it was this breadth and depth of skills that made the project succeed.

If you are setting up a garden with individual plots, there is still likely to be some work to be done both initially and on an ongoing basis. Collecting rents and keeping the books will not be onerous tasks, but they will still need to be done accurately and on time. Similarly, liaising with the landlord if you don't own the land and organizing community events will all go more smoothly if roles within the community are defined.

## Voluntary versus Paid

Most community gardens start with a group of willing, but unpaid,

volunteers. This usually means that they are rich in ideas and energy but often poor when it comes to devoting time. Many gardens survive and thrive purely on voluntary contributions, especially smaller enterprises and those with individual rented plots and simpler structures. However, for larger projects, it can be a struggle. If you are lucky, you might find someone who is able to help with your project as part of their day job. Better still, you might have money available to pay someone to help establish your garden.

Our community farm achieved a lot with volunteers, but it really took off when we were lucky enough to be given a sum of money by a generous individual. We employed someone two days a week for six months, and, at this point, the dream began to become a reality.

## Organizational Structure

Working by consensus is not always easy, but ultimately a community project needs to be run by the community. Even the simplest community garden will need some formal structure, and it is worth discussing how you want to work together as a group. This may seem like an indulgence, but it can really help. Set rules for how you want to run meetings and how often and who makes which decisions. Try to keep a balance between strong personalities and quieter ones, and make sure that all points of view are heard. Many good ideas are missed by groups that do not take time to properly consult with more introverted members.

ABOVE
Community gardens are a great way to bring people together, and experienced gardeners are often happy to pass on their knowledge to new gardeners of all ages.

# Raising Funds

Although small community gardens run by a few volunteers may not appear to need funding, most will. There are running costs, such as seeds, equipment, rent, and utility bills, as well as initial set-up costs. Capital investment may also be required at a later date. Community gardens with rented individual plots are probably the easiest to fund; the rental income can cover the running costs.

## Annual Fees

Whatever your garden structure, it is useful to have some regular income. This could be rental for individual plots, an annual membership fee, or income from weekly vegetable boxes. Deciding what to charge is not easy. You of course want to keep your project accessible to your community, but equally you need to ensure its long-term survival. Many projects offer reduced or free membership or rental to those who give time to help run the garden, and this can be a way of reducing costs and therefore how much income you need to generate.

## Informal Fundraising

Many gardening enterprises are able to generate income from the sale of their produce and plants or from bake sales and other types of small fundraising events. However, these avenues probably won't raise large sums and will often not be enough to cover additional expenditures. So, where do you get money for infrastructure, wages, purchasing or renting land, and other significant costs?

## Loans

If you are buying land, there may be options to get a mortgage secured on the real estate, but the bank will still need to be confident that you are able to meet the repayments. Smaller loans for setup costs can be arranged and perhaps secured by members or supporters of the project. Trusts and individuals may offer preferential terms to you that make this an attractive alternative. However, there is always a risk, and taking on debt at the start of a project can shackle it, preventing it from achieving its full potential.

## Share Offer

This is not for the fainthearted, but for larger projects that have real income

potential, you can raise large sums with share offers. There are ways of protecting the money raised to prevent investors from all withdrawing funds at the same time and leaving your project at risk. You will need guidance from someone with expertise and experience to launch a share offer.

## Crowdfunding

Crowdfunding is becoming a recognized way of raising money for projects of all sizes. It is an online phenomenon, and there are many platforms for crowdfunding that are relatively straightforward to use. A successful crowdfunding campaign may end up being a lot of hard work, however, so be aware of what you might be getting into.

## Applying for Grants

For capital items, wages for any hired garden helpers, or for funding some other charitable activity, it is worth finding out if there are any government grants or grants from trust funds available. Some funding will be available only to organizations with charitable status or community-interest companies (see pages 52-53).

## Financial Transparency

It is a good practice to set up a bank account and nominate a treasurer, even if you are only at the early planning stage. This will allow the group to be transparent and enforce the discipline of correct rigorous account management, which your group will need to embrace on an ongoing basis.

# How to Make Sure that Your Project Survives

Some community gardens spring up like morning glory—all lush and bright—only to fade just as quickly after a short burst. What can you do to make sure that your community garden grows into a mighty tree that will bear fruit for many years? Funding is important, of course, as is security of tenure on your land (see pages 50-51), but most vital is that you nurture the community itself.

People will come, and people will go. Families move on, and children are born and grow up. All of this changes who will be involved and how much time they will have to devote to your garden. Here are a few things to consider that might give your garden some tenacity.

## Start Small and Grow

Ambition is a wonderful thing, but so is patience. Getting too big, too quickly, can lead to debt, strain on the volunteers, neglect of the core purpose, and other problems that will risk the garden's survival. Even the fertility and health of your soil could be compromised if you push it too hard.

## Preserving Equality

One potentially tricky dynamic is those members of the group that have a special "status." This might be someone who has contributed a big chunk of money, the landowner, or the founder of the project, or just someone with strong opinions. While recognizing that the project would probably not have happened without these people, it is important to revisit the "community" aspect. It is easy to alienate sectors of your community by allowing a particular point of view to dominate.

## Revisit the Vision

Despite the risk of overanalyzing the situation, it's worth checking occasionally that everyone is still heading in the same direction, particularly for successful projects that grow rapidly. As members of a project focus on one area of work, it's easy to forget the rest of the project. Follow-up sessions could be held for the core team every six months or so, simply to run through the project objectives to make sure you are all still on track.

## Reliance on Funding

I strongly recommend not using temporary funding (such as short-term project grants) to pay wages or to fund your core activities. I have seen many projects fold because they relied too heavily on the project funding and did not develop a sustainable business model as a result. This might not be such an issue for inexpensive projects run by a small team of committed volunteers, but for a larger operation, it is vital that your core activities have a sustainable business model.

## Bringing in New Members

Whatever your model, replacing departing plot renters or members is vital to long-term survival. Sometimes thinking in business terms can be helpful. You might like to build a strategy for recruitment and retention. It can also be helpful to interview people when they leave to find out if you can improve the way you run your garden so that people might stay longer. It might be something simple, like a stricter policy on how plot renters should leave their patch when they move on. One garden I know decided to fundamentally change their volunteer setup up and work allocation to appeal to a different group of potential members.

ABOVE
Take time to celebrate the successes of the project. Include everyone who has been involved, whatever their contribution—every weed pulled and leaf picked will have made a difference.

# The Legalities: Land Tenure and Access

Gardening, growing and working on someone else's land requires their permission, and there are many ways of coming to an arrangement. Informal verbal agreements, for example, are quick and easy, and you can get started immediately without having to draw up legal documents. However, they leave you vulnerable to the whims of the owner, and although you might be able to move to an alternative site if you lose yours, it is much better to have some kind of security of tenure.

Drawing up a lease need not be long and complicated, and there are often templates available that suit the laws of a particular country or region. Ask around—other community gardens will probably share their experiences and rental agreements to help others like you. Most important, however, is to choose a landowner that you think is in it for the long term and appears to genuinely support the aims of your community. If he or she is just out to make a quick buck from renting out the land, then you may run into trouble. A few things to consider follow.

## Length of Lease

I would recommend trying to get a five-year lease, at the very least. The longer the better. If you are putting up tunnels, or planting even short-lived perennial plants, you need to know that you will see some benefit from it. You can insert clauses in the contract to allow either side to extricate themselves if the circumstances arise.

## Rental and Sub-Rental

If you are paying rent for the land, make sure you know how often and on what basis the rent will be reviewed. Also, make sure that you are clear about what is and isn't included. For example, does it include water, electricity, and insurance? If you are renting out individual plots, make sure your lease allows for this, that your plot sub-rental agreements match the rental agreement, and that your tenants understand their responsibilities.

## Who Pays for What?

Make sure it is clear who is responsible for what. Are you required to maintain fences and buildings? Who is required to make sure electrical or water supplies are safely maintained? Does the lease insist that you keep the site clean and tidy, and if so, what does this mean exactly?

## Make an Inventory

If any equipment is included in the lease, be sure that each item and its current state of repair are documented. Make an inventory of everything: fences, walkways or paved areas, landscaped areas, machinery, and anything else that might be relevant. The landowner may require you to replace or repair damaged property.

## Access

If you need to cross someone else's land to get to your site, do you have permission to do so? Is this for vehicles as well as on foot? Do others have rights of access over the land that you will be using, and, if so, during what hours of the day or night? Will parking cause problems for neighbours on busy volunteer or open days? Do you have enough room for parking?

## Be Open

Be clear and open with the landowner about what you want to do on the site. Ask if he or she agrees to having trees planted, and, if so, what size? If your aim in the long term is to offer community-service opportunities, declare this at the start. The landlord may require you to observe certain restrictions to be observed if they are unhappy, so you should put everything on the table to avoid unpleasant surprises later on.

## Improvements

If, through the activities and investment of the community garden, work is done that makes the site more valuable, find out if you will be compensated at the end of the arrangement. Also, if the rent is reviewed, any improvements that the community project has paid for should be disregarded so that you are not paying more rent because you have made the land more valuable.

## Statutory Terms

The law makes certain provision for agricultural tenancies, whether or not they are contained in an agreement between a landlord and tenant. It is worth finding out about these to know your rights and obligations.

ABOVE
What trees you can plant may be restricted by the landowner so do make sure you clear your plans for how your community garden intends to use the land with them.

# Legal Structures for Community Enterprises

Small projects may decide to keep things informal, but for most groups, a legal structure is advisable. In fact, if you are applying for funding or employing helpers, it is essential that you exist as a legal organization. In many countries, this would be as an "unincorporated association," which can operate as either for- or not-for profit. Even if you decide to operate without a formal legal structure, you will still be defined in law.

Depending on in which country or state the community garden is set up, there will be a range of legal structures potentially open to your group. With a resurgence of interest in community-owned projects worldwide, this is a constantly developing area. I won't try to go into detail about particular constitutions, but I will try instead to suggest what will affect your decision and some of the consequences of choosing the different types of setup.

Keep in mind that the legal structure of the organization and how it is run day-to-day are not the same. For example, the project could be registered as a limited, for-profit company, and yet be owned and run as a workers' cooperative, with consensual decision-making and equal pay for all.

## For-Profit Options

You can run the project as a sole operator, as a partnership, or as a limited-liability (LLC) company. The first two are relatively easy to set up, but it does means that you (individually or as partners) are personally responsible for any losses or debt that the community garden makes. LLCs, on the other hand, have shareholders who own the business and directors who are responsible for running it. Directors and shareholders can be the same people, but they don't have to be. The shareholders' financial liability is limited to the amount they've invested. The directors' liability is limited so long as they act within the law and in good faith.

With LLCs, a share of any profits will be distributed among the shareholders, with an agreed amount remaining in the company's bank account for the day-to-day running of the project

and to cover any future investments. The shareholders can decide to use the profits toward the charitable or community aims of your group, although you would need a separate agreement with the board to this effect.

## Not-for-Profit Options

Non-profit corporations are organizations with limited liability, and they do not exist to distribute profits to shareholders. Instead, they use any trading surplus to further specific social or environmental aims. They have greater flexibility in what they do and how they operate than charities do, and the regulation of them is more straightforward.

If the financial activities of the community garden will be exclusively charitable and are big enough to benefit from tax relief, then forming a charity may be an option. It may make the project eligible for grants and funding available only to charities. However, the drawback is that charities must engage in only charitable activity, with restrictions placed on their wider activities.

## A Compromise

In recent years, a growing phenomenon known as "B Corps" has begun to spread around the world. A "B Corp"—shorthand for "benefit corporation"—is a for-profit company that chooses to put governance arrangements in place that explicitly state that it will give social and environmental considerations equal weight to financial returns when taking business decisions. Other types of setups may also offer viable options. As always, ask around and do your research to discover what will be the most suitable option.

**LEFT**
Even small community gardens on publicly owned land, such as raised beds, should consider which type of enterprise is best for their particular group and its needs.

# Community Events

Organizing events is a crucial aspect of most community gardens. The events you run are especially important for gardens that are made up of individual plots because they will be the main activities that bring members together. They can also attract new supporters, volunteers, or plot renters and can help raise funds for your garden.

Each event will be different, and you should consider carefully what the objectives of the day should be and to whom you are aiming it—for example, children, adults, or people with learning difficulties. People love learning new skills, particularly in an environment they are familiar with, surrounded by people they know.

## Planning and Learning

Community events can be incredibly wide-ranging, so where do you begin? Horticultural training events are a good first step, but think beyond this to imagine anything your members might be interested in. Whatever you choose to do, you should plan well enough in advance to publicize the event, book speakers, rent or borrow equipment, and so on. Last-minute events can result in either no one showing up or the event's being chaotic and disorganized. Keep in mind that it is also easy to overcomplicate events. You start with one idea, but an excess of enthusiasm or seemingly unmissable

opportunities can derail your original plans or cause your budget to spiral. Remember that from one idea may come many more—so put them aside and save them for another time instead of trying to cram everything into the one event.

## Horticultural Events

Some thoughts for horticultural training or events include seed sowing, plant propagation, pruning, seed saving, compost making, soil management, making your own hand tools, building and growing on a hotbed, designing a vegetable plot, and growing herbs. There are, of course, many more. For most subjects, a balanced mix of theory and practical works well. Prepare a handout so that people have something they can take away with them.

Think ahead. If you're doing a grafting workshop, for example, you may need to order rootstocks well in advance to make sure they are available for the day. Do you have the right equipment?

If twenty people come to a course and have to share the three blunt and rusty knives from the corner of the tool shed, they'll be disappointed. You can ask people to bring their own tools, or, if a special piece of equipment is needed, you can include the cost in the price of the course or offer it for sale at the event.

Does your garden have the facilities to run the event? Outdoor practical training can be miserable if it rains all day and there is nowhere to take shelter for a drink. Having a space to do some indoor teaching will add to the range of educational events you will be able to run. And always remember to complete health and safety forms for a successful day.

## A Sample Course Timetable

This is an example agenda for an apple grafting course that I ran for a community farm.

| | |
|---|---|
| **10:00** | Arrive for refreshments |
| **10:15** | Theory of grafting: history and science; how to choose rootstocks and varieties |
| **11:00** | Selection and cutting of scion wood; this also allows for you to do a tour of the garden and show people how the trees are growing |
| **12:00** | Lunch |
| **1:00** | Theory of techniques |
| **1:30** | Practical: actually doing it |
| **2:45** | Summing up and celebration of having created some trees |

**ABOVE**
Learning how to sow and plant are easy skills that require little equipment. However, it's good to have some ground already prepared.

# Seed-Swap Event

Seed swaps are not only great for getting free seeds, they also bring in a wider community than your core volunteer, plot renter, or committee member. The events can be as simple or as complicated as you want. Although people have been swapping seeds for as long as they have been growing plants, organized seed-swap events have grown greatly in popularity since the turn of the millennium.

Seed swaps are also an opportunity to raise awareness about food sovereignty and the decline of our agricultural biodiversity. The United Nations Food and Agriculture Organization has estimated that we have already lost 75 percent of our genetic diversity on farms. Special breeds and heirloom varieties are disappearing fast because they are no longer commercially viable for large-scale agriculture.

Community gardens can help reverse this decline through practical action and education. By growing rare and heirloom varieties, particularly those that are part of your local heritage or well-suited to your local conditions, community gardens can do their part to help keep the diversity alive.

## Swapping Knowledge

As well as the physical seeds, ideas and knowledge are also exchanged during seed swaps. Print simple fact sheets on growing particular crops or varieties as well as tips on how to save the seeds.

Another good way to share know-how is to hold a "Gardeners' Q&A" panel featuring local gardeners. Practical demonstrations of collecting, cleaning, and storing seeds also do well.

## Advance Preparation

Preparation starts well before the actual day. You and other potential seed savers need plenty of advance warning to collect seeds. Ideally, you should start the planning one year in advance. You'll probably find a lot of people are saving seeds anyway, so don't panic.

Set some quality guidelines right from the start. Make sure that people know to save seeds from only open-pollinated varieties (that is, from plants that aren't hybrids). Consider creating label templates for seed packets so that all the information is comparable. The more information people can give about the seeds the better; for example, the number of plants they were collected from, the proximity of other varieties of the same family when the seeds were collected (this may affect the purity of the seeds), the date of collection, and the number of years that the collector has been saving seeds of this variety.

## What Is the Law?

Current global seed laws that favour multinational corporations are part of the reason why biodiversity is declining. However, it is important to know what the law is before you decide whether or not to break it.

You should not save seeds from varieties registered with Patents or Plant Breeders Rights. To be on the safe side look for varieties whose license has expired. It is also important not to bring plants or seeds from abroad or from the wild which could carry pests and diseases harmful to our native flora and fauna.

## A Few Practicalities

In the first year or two, you may have more people wanting seeds than those able to offer them. See if you can get donations from more established seed swaps, or find a commercial supplier of seeds that is willing to sell seeds at your event, particularly a local or specialty supplier. This means that people will not go home disappointed. Think also about how the seeds might be distributed. Will the seed collectors pack up their own seeds? Or will you pour seeds into large containers so that people can help themselves and put some into an envelope? If so, make sure that you come equipped with plenty of envelopes and pens.

# Skill-Share Events

You will certainly have a range of skills within your network. Beekeepers, basket weavers, cooks, wildlife experts or crafters can all bring their skills to your community garden. You may need to approach your members or plot renters individually to find out what skills they have. Framing these events as "skill shares" can help make the prospect less scary for those not used to speaking in public.

Although there is a wealth of information and videos available on the Internet that you can use to learn new skills, there's nothing like being shown something in real life and then trying it out with someone on hand to help you get it right. Framing a skill-share event as a social occasion also turns it into a fun day out instead of strictly educational.

## Plan the Day

How the event is organized depends on whether the day is focused around one skill or many. A day devoted to beekeeping, for example, might involve a local beekeeper sharing his or her experiences and skills, perhaps with the opportunity for the group to practice honey extraction or putting a hive together. This approach could attract a large group of people who are eager to learn about that particular subject, but, conversely, it may be limited in appeal.

Alternatively, a full day could be organized with one-hour slots for demonstrating different types of skills. This way, each person can offer one skill but learn many more in return. It will take a little more effort to organize, and, in particular, it means finding more skilled people; however, this approach will feel more like a community event with people sharing and learning all day long.

## Sharing Skills, Sharing Food

To add something extra to the event and to get people talking, organize a nice lunch or buffet for the people coming to your skill share. Keep it as simple as possible—for example, bread and cheese, or a stew or soup—or ask the participants to be part of a potluck and bring a dish each to share.

Through the generosity and kindness of members, the food rarely runs short, even if a few people forget to bring something. You may also be pleasantly surprised to find that the people you have been working with have hidden culinary skills that they are eager to share with the group.

**LEFT**
Try to have a range of different activities at the skill-share event so that everyone can get involved.

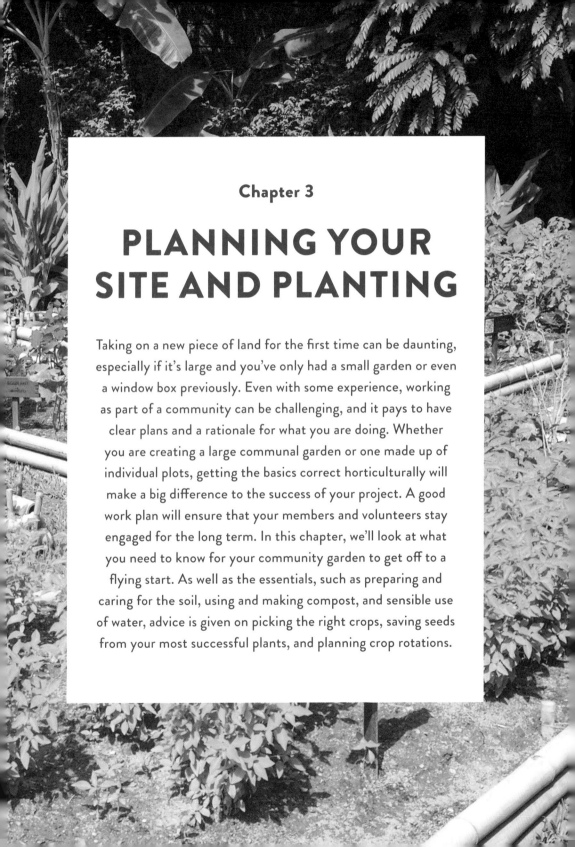

### Chapter 3

# PLANNING YOUR SITE AND PLANTING

Taking on a new piece of land for the first time can be daunting, especially if it's large and you've only had a small garden or even a window box previously. Even with some experience, working as part of a community can be challenging, and it pays to have clear plans and a rationale for what you are doing. Whether you are creating a large communal garden or one made up of individual plots, getting the basics correct horticulturally will make a big difference to the success of your project. A good work plan will ensure that your members and volunteers stay engaged for the long term. In this chapter, we'll look at what you need to know for your community garden to get off to a flying start. As well as the essentials, such as preparing and caring for the soil, using and making compost, and sensible use of water, advice is given on picking the right crops, saving seeds from your most successful plants, and planning crop rotations.

# New Plot, What Now?

Plots of land always have their defining characteristics, and it will take time to develop an understanding of what your new plot can and cannot offer. Some things you will be able to grow well; others, not so well. You will learn as you go, but there are a few things you can do before you begin that will help you assess the potential of your site and get off to a great start.

## Soil

The first thing to do is get intimately acquainted with your soil. Understanding your soil is a key to success. Practical tests like rolling a bit of soil in your hand can tell you the proportion of sand, silt or clay particles in your soil; sandy soils will feel gritty, while heavy clay can be rolled into a sticky ball. However, when taking on a new site it is also worth getting a simple lab test done to highlight any potential nutrient imbalances. For urban sites you can also ask the lab to test for potential soil contamination such as lead. If you are taking on a site that has not recently had crops, then you might need to do more than if you are taking over a plot with a known history. Before you plant anything, dig a few test holes, look at the depth of the topsoil, and do a soil test to find out if there are any hidden problems. You are looking for significant deficiencies or excesses of nutrients. Some urban or ex-industrial sites might have severely contaminated ground, in which case your only option would be to grow in raised beds, above ground level.

## Get Wet

It's useful to know if any part of the site floods, and the best way to find out is to visit after a day or so of heavy rain. Mark out with sticks any areas that are sitting in water. Revisit after a day and again after three days to see how quickly the water drains away. Short-term puddling may not be an issue, but long-term flooding will cause problems, and you may need to break up the subsoil, add drainage, or, at worst, give up production on that part of the plot.

## Ask Your Neighbours

Although this may not help in urban areas, asking local growers for their experience is a great and usually

free way to understand more about your site. They may even know the history of the site and what grew well previously. Hang out with the local gardening club, or knock on doors near the site. People are often delighted to share memories and knowledge.

## Work With Your Limitations

Plots of land are never perfect. There are always limitations, and once you find out what they are, you can work around them or even turn them into strengths. For example, if your plot is small, you will have to make decisions about which crops to grow and which ones to leave out. If it is too large, you must resist the urge to grow more

crops than you have the time, money, and equipment for.

Other challenges you may face could include the aspects of the site, such as being steep or not facing the sun. One factor that is never readily appreciated is the microclimate; over time you will discover whether there are any frost pockets, wind tunnels, and sun traps. If you are splitting your garden into individual plots, you will have to find a fair way of deciding who gets the best spots in the garden. Some community gardens have arrangements in which existing plot holders have the opportunity to upgrade to a better plot before it is offered to new members.

**ABOVE**
What you grow and where you grow it can be determined by the type of soil: sandy soil drains quickly and becomes dry in hot weather, while heavy clay soil can become waterlogged. Loam, with a mixture of sand, silt, and clay, is the best type of soil for growing healthy plants.

# Planning the layout

Consult your members and begin to draw up a detailed plan of how you want to lay out the garden. It may take time to make sure different people's needs and expectations are taken into consideration. As well as deciding which crops to grow, think about ease of access, potential trading operations, staff requirements, health and safety, car parking, and security.

Many factors will affect the final layout of a community garden. The scale of the site can determine how many paths are needed, and the condition of the soil might suggest the use of raised beds. Community needs might also dictate how high these raised beds are and their size. If you have a tractor, the paths will need to be of a certain width. Put it together piece by piece.

## Buildings and Social Areas

Your garden may require covered structures, such as a propagation area or tool shed. Even in a plot-based community garden, you may want to have a shared space for meetings, activities, and shelter, and you will need to factor this into the budget. If theft is a possible problem, consider a secure unit where the gardeners can store their tools or hide and disguise a tool shed behind trees or shrubs.

## Which Crops?

Deciding what to grow, and where to grow it, is mainly a horticultural choice, but other factors can come into play. Where are the access points, and which crops will you want to reach all year round? What about the water supply? If yours is a plot-based system, this will obviously be up to individual members. For small groups, the choice of crops can be a community decision. For larger communities, it is best to delegate to the grower and adjust the selection as time goes by and preferences become known.

## Plants Prefer Rainwater

If you can use the roofs of buildings, greenhouses, or tunnels to collect rainwater, you will improve your carbon footprint and potentially reduce costs aside from filters and pumps. If possible, site your water collection at the top of a slope—gravity reduces energy costs. One of the surprising things about growing on a larger scale is how much water is needed. Can you manage with watering cans or a hose? Drip or overhead watering systems are useful, but they will increase costs up front.

**OPPOSITE TOP**
Using a rough sketch to plan your garden is a great way of exploring different layouts. Before you commit to a final design, try marking out the various options you come up with on the ground with stakes, so you get a better idea of how your ideas might work in practice.

**OPPOSITE BOTTOM**
When planning a garden that will be divided into individual plots, think about which resources will be shared and ensure that everyone has easy access to them.

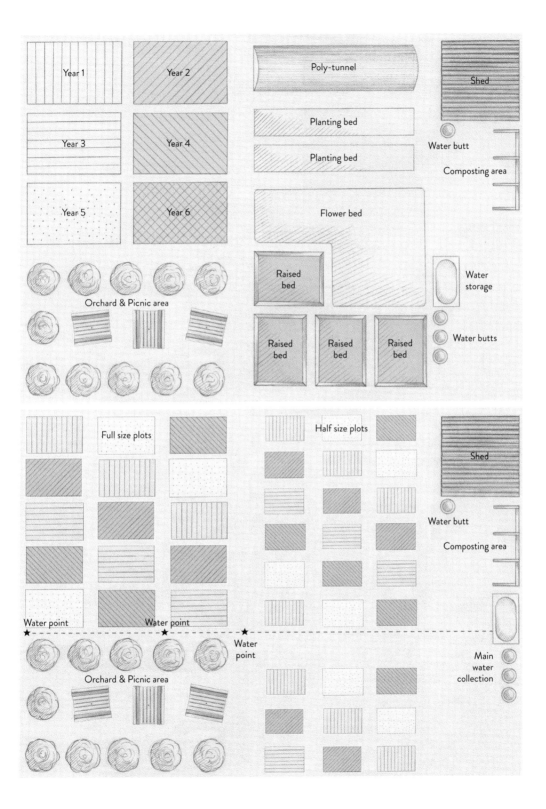

## Greenhouses and Tunnels

Growing plants under glass or plastic is not essential, but it will certainly lengthen the growing season and extend the variety of crops that can be grown. The choice of material largely depends on budget. Here are a few tips on where to place them:

› For individual plots, decide whether you will allow protected cropping structures on each plot.
› If your site is sloped, run them up and down instead of sideways.

The change in gradient encourages airflow that helps reduce disease.
› Don't erect them in the shade; your protected planting space is your most valuable growing area, so don't compromise it. For instance, you will lose a one percent yield of tomatoes for every one percent loss of light.
› Put them near the entrance, if possible, for easier access for harvesting in the winter.

**LEFT AND ABOVE**
Tunnels offer protection to your crops against extreme weather conditions, allowing you to extend the growing season and grow some crops that would not thrive outside.

# Preparing the Ground

The health of your soil should be part of your long-term plan. Starting with maximum planting can cause problems further down the line. Instead, make provision for the soil's fertility and accept that you might lose some production in the short term. Here are some ideas on how to prepare the ground for planting at different times of the year, depending on when you get access to the land.

Some techniques will only be applicable to small-scale gardeners. Others might not be possible without a particular type of machinery. Pick the ones that suit your situation and scale. If you haven't used power machinery before, be aware that it has the potential to damage soil.

## Summer to Early Autumn

There is little that can be planted at this time of year. The best strategy is to use this opportunity to get in a really good, fertility-building "green manure" or cover crop. Prepare the ground by digging and raking, or ploughing, and sow a mixture of legumes, fibrous grasses, and deep rooters, such as chicory or tillage radish. This will start improving the soil immediately. If you don't plan to cultivate the area for several years, a perennial cover crop could be used, but they can be harder to remove in the long run.

## Late Autumn to Early Spring

Late autumn is too late in most climates to get a good cover crop sown.

In smaller-scale gardens, you can cover the ground with cardboard and mulch with a layer of compost. This will kill many of the annual weeds over winter and give you a clear bed in spring, which can be quickly worked over with a fork or a tractor with tines. Cut back any existing plants as short as possible with a hoe, grass trimmer or flail mower before mulching. Leave the cut material on the surface, it will decompose into the soil over winter.

## Late Spring to Early Summer

At this time of year, you will naturally want to start growing plants immediately, so unless your soil is in really poor condition, you can dig areas and plant as you need them. For larger areas, it's worth getting the whole plot ploughed and prepared with machinery and sowing cover crops on the areas you won't be cultivating immediately. Short-term cover crops, such as mustards or phacelia, are ideal for areas you will need in the near future, and longer-term leas should be sown for parts of the rotation that will be left for a few years before they are cultivated.

RIGHT
Although planting an area with a cover crop will mean that it will be temporarily unavailable for growing your harvest, it is a good way of improving the soil to yield a healthy crop in future months or years.

# When to Replace or Improve Your Soil

If you are establishing a community garden on a site with no soil, or you are unable to use the soil because it is unusable or contaminated, you will need to bring in some topsoil or soil mix to grow your plants in. Splitting into individual plots or growing communal raised beds are both great ways of creating manageable growing spaces without soil.

Finding a good supplier of topsoil and soil mix is crucial and not always easy. For smaller pots, the whole container will need to be filled with a good soil mix, but you can save money with larger containers or raised beds by using lower-grade materials in the bottom layer.

Spend time researching and devising a good design for your containers. There are some smart systems, such as wicking beds, that use gravel to help reduce the need for watering. Other innovations for raised beds include hugelkultur and keyhole gardens.

## Matching Compost to Crops

Keep in mind that different plants have different needs, so save the best soil mix for the plants that need a rich substrate. For instance, a fruit bush can be planted in a coarser soil mix than that needed for sowing seeds. If you can find a local tree surgeon who needs to get rid of chipped wood, you can compost this and use it either as a mulch for larger pots or, when it has broken down, as soil mix. You can check out my Woodchip Handbook for more details.

## Buying Commercial Soil

Reputable suppliers will be able to give you an analysis of their soil mix or topsoil. Check for levels of heavy metals. If possible, find out where the soil came from in the first place, although not all suppliers will know. A bad substrate will probably contain impurities, weed seeds, and—in the worst cases—fragments of noxious perennial weeds.

## Contamination

In some countries, garden and yard waste is collected and composted. It can be a good source of cheap substrate, but there is a risk of contamination.

The material will probably have been screened at the facility, but contaminants, such as glass and plastic, may still be present as small particles not visible to the naked eye.

There are also some weed killers (aminopyralid and clopyralid) that are used on grass and broad-leafed weeds. They can survive the composting process and harm your crops once planted. You can test the substrate by sowing bean seeds in it. These plants are sensitive to weed killers, and any distortion in their growth can be a sure sign that herbicides are present.

## Improving Your Soil

If good-quality topsoil or soil mix is unavailable in your area, or just too expensive, you may have to revisit the idea of growing in your own soil. Unless your land is severely contaminated, it is possible to build most soil—no matter how poor it is—into good soil using a lot of well-aged compost, but it can take time and dedication, and your planting will be limited in the short to medium term. A substance known as biochar has been shown to help clean up contaminated soil by locking up some of the heavy metals and making them unavailable to plant roots.

**ABOVE**
Raised beds don't have to cost the community garden a fortune. You can use natural materials to create custom-made features that suit their surroundings and are also the exact size you require.

# Watering

Plants need water to grow, and the occasional rain shower cannot be relied upon to give a community garden enough water to produce healthy plants and good yields. Even if the soil is good and deep, you will need some extra water, and if you are growing under cover or in containers, you will need a lot of it. This is a fundamental question for any community garden: how will it be irrigated?

The best place to get water is from the sky—it is free and usually purer than tap water. However, the rain can't be turned on and off when you need it, so other options such as boreholes and tap water must be considered. You may also decide to grow crops that cope well with less water.

Design a planting plan to suit water availability and predicted use. If water is limited, you may have to ration it and choose vegetables that can cope with limited watering, or allocate an annual water allowance to each plot holder. Giving each plot its own tap will make it easier but will also encourage greater use of water. Shared taps can encourage more frugal use of water.

## Watering Routines

Watering little and often encourages roots to stay at the surface, making the plants vulnerable to drought. A really good soak every week until the soil is wet to a depth of at least 10 cm (4 inches) encourages the roots to dig deeper, which means that the plants will be more likely to survive if you are unable to water for a short time, and is a more sustainable use of water as less is lost to evaporation. Crops may need slightly more when they are newly planted, but consistency is key.

## Which Watering System?

The scale and setup of your community garden will determine how you go about delivering the water to your plants. The main pipes will need to service, at a minimum, a few key points or, if you want to supply individual plots, you may need a more complicated system. Aim to place points along paths or garden edges where the ground is less likely to be disturbed.

You then need to decide how to get the water to the plants. For small gardens, individual plots, or those just starting out, a garden hose is an inexpensive option that works even with low water pressure. However, it can be time consuming during dry periods, and it is difficult to control how much water each plant gets.

**TOP**
The "rose" attachment prevents damage to delicate plants and seedlings.

**MIDDLE**
Hoses are a good option for smaller gardens.

**BOTTOM**
Drip irrigation systems with individual nozzles as shown or leaky pipe provide efficient and economical water-use.

Larger gardens will benefit from an automated watering system. Drip systems are a relatively efficient way of delivering water because less water is wasted, but they are more expensive to set up and can get in the way of crop management, such as hoeing. Overhead systems are cheaper to set up but use more water. They are usually installed in tunnels or greenhouses with an overhead structure to attach them to, but fungal disease may be a problem on some crops if their leaves get too wet. Soaker hoses or drip tape are good for closely spaced plants, such as lettuce. For larger plants, such as tomatoes, use a drip nozzle for each plant for more efficient and effective watering.

## What is Wrong with Tap Water?

Many gardens rely on tap water because it is clean and reliable However, there are several reasons why you might not want to use it:

> It is expensive and is usually paid for per unit.
> It often contains chlorine, fluoride, and sodium, added for the benefit of the humans who drink it. However, these additives are not necessarily good for plant health.
> In some areas, tap water is hard with a high pH, which is not good for most plants.
> There is a small but significant amount of nitrogen (which is good for plant growth) in rain, but not in tap water.

Two good alternatives to tap water are to store rainwater (see pages 74-75) or, if it is legal in your area, to sink a well or drill a borehole; drilling down to the water table will access clean and filtered water. The water will need to be pumped up to ground level. However, it is expensive, and usually worthwhile only for larger operations.

# Water Harvesting

There are many advantages to be had from collecting and storing water, particularly rainwater, which plants prefer. Using this free resource is not only good for your plants, it is also much less wasteful than tap water, which is costly and has an associated environmental cost (processing and cleaning tap water uses a lot of energy). Harvesting water during heavy rain can also help prevent flooding.

## How to Harvest Rainwater

Rainwater is most easily collected from the roofs of existing buildings. In many situations, these roofs will already be fitted with gutters that can be diverted to a storage container. Run a pipe, if necessary. Most tunnels and greenhouses can be fitted with gutters, and these will, of course, be exactly where the water is needed. It is possible to collect water runoff and rain from higher ground into a purpose-built collecting area. This can be a cheap method, but it will also give you the dirtiest water.

## Potential Water Supply

Decide on the area you'll be collecting from, and find out the average monthly rainfall in your location. You might get about 1 litre per m² for each 1 mm of rain that falls (0.6 gallon per square foot for each inch), of which you might lose one-quarter before you get to use it. The following formulas allow you to calculate your potential annual water supply.

IN GALLONS:
Area (square feet) x 0.6 x 75% of annual rainfall (inches)

IN LITRES:
Area (m²) x 75% of annual rainfall (mm)

## Storing Water

When it comes to storing water, small community gardens and plot holders may be able to make do using

salvaged water barrels, or other closed watertight containers. Larger gardens will almost certainly need to invest in more robust and costly infrastructure. There can still be advantages in storing tap water—the chlorine will evaporate, for instance, and tanks can be filled at night when not as much water is being used and pressure is normally higher.

Deciding how big a storage tank to buy is difficult, but being able to store at least one week's supply is useful. Use your local weather data to calculate how much water you might collect in a seven-day period, and get a tank that will store that amount.

## Water Delivery

In a small garden, a watering can is a fine water delivery tool, provided you have the labour. On a larger scale, you will certainly need a hose, and possibly an automated watering system (see pages 72–73). You may need to invest in a pump. The capacity of the pump will depend on how much water is needed, how far it needs to travel, and the pumping gradient.

## Water Quality

Be aware that contamination can be a risk when stored water is used for irrigating ready-to-eat crops, such as salad greens, or for growing seedlings or propagating new plants. In these cases, the water will need to be filtered to avoid being a potential hazard. In rural areas, there is also a risk of chemical contamination of your water supply from drift or runoff from neighbouring farmers who use herbicides and pesticides. It is extemely imporant that water-storage tanks are covered. This not only prevents debris, such as fallen leaves, from falling into them, but it also keeps insects, such as disease-carrying mosquitoes, from breeding.

**ABOVE**
Any watertight container can be used to collect and harvest rainwater.

**LEFT**
You can fit a gutter to almost any garden structure, letting you collect rainwater in your chosen container.

# Building a Shed

Many community gardens decide to set up a communal area for the garden or for individual renters to share. Having a structure gives, at the bare minimum, a place to hang a few tools, store work clothes, or take shelter from the rain. It can also be a place to gather with fellow gardeners to discuss the day's work, to bemoan the weather, or to admire how much you all have achieved.

Instead of buying an expensive shed, you can build a strong and waterproof shelter from recycled materials. Most community groups will have a member with some carpentry experience, and that certainly helps, but even if that is not the case, don't be put off. Building a structure as a group, and learning by doing so, is a great team-building experience, and you will feel so proud every time you use it.

## Building a Pallet Shed

What you'll need:
› A lot of pallets, ideally of the same size.
› Concrete blocks or solid bricks to form the base.
› Long lumber pieces (you may be able to reclaim them): 4x4 lengths for the uprights and 2x4 lengths for the roof frame.
› Board and builder's felt covering, or sheet roofing metal, for the roof.
› Board for the outside of the shed—cheap plywood, reclaimed tongue-and-groove, or other salvaged material can be used; you can even make your own panelling from reclaimed pallets.
› Heavy-duty nuts and bolts to hold the pallets together.

## The Frame

Pallets are relatively small, so you need to create a strong frame to fit them into. You can either build a self-supporting frame that sits on a firm base, or you can concrete or secure your corner posts firmly into the ground. The latter will be stronger, but the posts will eventually rot at the base, so you may need to replace the shed sooner.

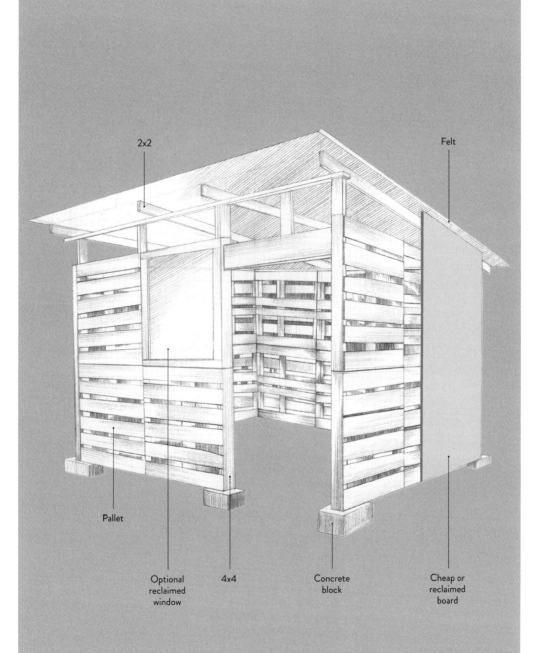

2x2

Felt

Pallet

Optional
reclaimed
window

4x4

Concrete
block

Cheap or
reclaimed
board

## The Base

You need to raise the base off the ground to keep it dry. This is easily done by laying concrete blocks or solid bricks at intervals and then laying your pallets on top. If your ground is soft, dig out a hole under each block and fill with rammed-down hardcore, such as stones or broken bricks. Make sure the blocks are perfectly level, or you might have an angled shed.

## Walls, Doors, and Windows

These are made by pallets stacked on their ends and secured to the frame with heavy-duty bolts. You will need one upright in the frame every two or three pallets to keep the shed secure.

## The Roof and Panelling

Once the walls are up, secure a roof frame on top. Flat roofs are simpler to construct but usually have a shorter lifespan. Give it at least a 10-degree pitch to ensure good drainage from the roof into your water collection system. The final touch is to cover the exterior walls of the shed with your chosen panelling material. The aim is to make sure the whole structure is waterproof and weather resistant.

LEFT AND ABOVE
Sheds can be of almost any size and complexity, depending on the materials you have and your ambition.

# Nutrition: Soil

The state of the soil in your community garden will probably be one of your greatest assets, and, as a result, it needs to be nurtured and continually improved. Like people, plants need food to live and thrive, and to get the best out of your crops, you must feed the soil. The plants will take what they need through their roots; everything else sustains a complex web of soil organisms that keep the soil "alive."

## Organic Gardening

This differs from the artificial amendments approach, which uses a range of artificially produced nutrients believed to match the requirements of a particular crop. Although using chemicals can work well in the short term, over time it often leads to a decline in soil organic matter and health and a breakdown in the growing system. Nitrogen is particularly hard to manage. It is vital for crop growth but soluble and hard to bring into your system and hold onto. This is why the cornerstone of many organic systems is to grow legumes within the garden, which collect nitrogen from the soil via bacterial relations (see opposite).

## Adding Organic Matter

Building soil organic matter is one of the main ways to improve the fertility of your soil. Not only will it provide some nutrients in itself, but it also encourages a greater number and diversity of soil organisms; as they eat each other and excrete, they will become a source of food for plants. The addition of good-quality aged compost to the soil is the best way of increasing organic matter, but composted wood chips, farmyard manure, mushroom compost, and biochar are all good materials if you have access to them.

## Fertility-Building Crops

This is a term used for plants that are not harvested but grown to increase fertility and to rest the soil. They are sometimes called "cover crops" or "green manure" and can be block-sown on areas that are lying unused (long-term mixtures are described on page 68) or sown under other crops to protect the soil from both physical damage and nutrient leaching in heavy rain. An example might be to sow low-growing legumes, such as clover, underneath larger crops, such as squash or brassicas (cabbage-family plants).

Deep-rooting plants, such as chicory or forage radish, are sometimes grown as a way of accessing nutrients that otherwise would be locked up in the

lower levels of the soil. Rotating crops, so that crops are moved around from year to year, will also help balance and maintain the soil's fertility (see pages 90–91). Comfrey is a great deep-rooted plant, and the leaves, which contain all these nutrients, can be soaked to produce a plant food. Be careful to buy a sterile cultivar such as 'Bocking-14'.

## Holding onto Fertility

Getting food for your plants is only half the battle—you also need to keep it. The organic content of the soil is especially important in this respect, because it acts like a sponge, holding water and the nutrients that

are dissolved in it. If you let the soil become compacted, the pores of this "sponge" will be destroyed, so treat your soil with respect.

## Supplements

In certain circumstances, it may be necessary to add supplementary nutrients to the soil. Micronutrients can be added with a single dose; I suggest adding them to the compost pile and then spreading the enriched compost over your ground. Extreme pH levels can also cause an imbalance of certain nutrients because some of them become unavailable or "locked up" if the pH is too acidic or alkaline.

# Nutrition: Containers

Only with the largest containers or raised beds is it possible to manage a long-term fertility strategy for your soil. Most container growing is, therefore, for the short term, and it relies on a good-quality soil mix that will need to be replenished from time to time. Some of the heavier feeding crops will need supplementary feeding through the season, and the soil mix should stay moist at all times.

## Liquid Feeding

However good the growing medium, some crops will need some extra nutrients to give you the optimum yield, particularly if they are growing in small containers. For example, tomatoes need a lot of potassium once they start producing fruit, and a small weekly application of a fertilizer will ensure that the crop doesn't run out of steam.

Plant-based fertilizers are readily available, or you can make your own from plants that are naturally high in potassium, such as comfrey. Keep a close eye on your plants and look for signs of discoloration in the leaves or problems with the fruits. Refer to a nutrient-deficiency chart to check what these symptoms might mean because the plant is probably trying to tell you something.

## Growing Trees in Containers

When growing deep-rooted trees in large containers, it is vital that there is enough long-term fertility and structure in the soil. Such plants prefer a substrate that is dominated by fungi (as opposed to bacteria), and the lignin-heavy content of a well-rotted wood-chip compost should provide this. It will also give the necessary structure and prevent the soil mix from slumping.

## Holding onto Nutrients

Most nutrients that a plant needs will be dissolved in the water in the soil mix. Therefore, if the soil mix is kept moist, the nutrients that the crops need will be available. Overwatering, however, has the reverse effect, because it will probably wash the nutrients out of the soil.

Organic matter in aged compost does the job of holding water in the soil, but there are other additives, such as biochar, that have a similar effect. Biochar is a form of charcoal formulated for growing; it has a huge surface area and can suck up large amounts of water, which it then slowly releases back out to plants as they need it. It also provides within its honeycomb structure a safe place for microorganisms to reside when it gets dry, which makes any growing medium that contains biochar more biologically resilient.

## Recycling Your Soil Mix

Soil mix can be reused from one year to the next, but be aware that it quickly becomes exhausted of nutrients and there is a risk of disease carrying over. I would recommend not using old soil mix for the same crop, but you can rotate it as you would do with crops in the open ground. Also look out for the grubs of the vine weevil, which thrive in undisturbed containers. These pests can do a lot of damage, undetected as they munch through plant roots.

# Composting

"Compost" is a term that can mean different things to different people. The soil mix in which container plants are grown is called compost in some countries, but most gardeners use the term to refer to the stuff you get when you take organic materials through the composting process. It is sometimes called "garden compost," and you will think of it as gold when you see what wonders it can do for your soil.

Well-aged compost is a great source of organic matter. Added to the soil or to container plants, it will boost biological activity, suppress disease, and result in stronger, healthier plants with better yields.

A compost pile is an excellent way of processing all the organic waste that is generated through the year, and, for this reason alone, it is why every community garden should have one. Larger sites should be able to make enough space to do composting really well, collecting material from around the site or from all plot renters into one composting area.

## Equipment

Well-rotted compost can be made in a simple covered heap, turning it backwards and forwards every couple of months so that the materials mix well and the bugs can get to work. This can be a little messy, though, so in small community gardens or urban situations, it makes sense to have a contained compost heap. There are

many commercial ones, or you can make one from old pallets or other reclaimed wood. It helps to have at least two compost areas side by side, so that the material can occasionally be turned from one to the other.

## Compost Ingredients

Theoretically, almost anything of organic origin can be put through the composting process, but in urban areas, you have to be careful about attracting vermin. Stick to adding garden waste, paper and cardboard, and fruit and vegetable scraps. Woody material needs to be shredded or chipped before composting. You will need an even mixture of both woody and non–woody material to make good compost.

Young annual weeds are fine to add as long as they have not gone to seed. However, do not add perennial weeds, because they can survive in the pile and multiply once you put the compost back onto the soil. Avoid any grains (bread, couscous, and so on), meat, and cooked food. Although there are ways of dealing with these (such as with the bokashi composting method), you will not be the most popular member of your community group if you're the one who brings the rats in.

## Time

Compost can be ready in as little as six weeks, but it usually takes longer. Regular turning makes sure that all parts of the pile are evenly composted and that it doesn't get too hot during the process, which can kill off the essential aerobic bacteria. When the compost has transformed into a black and crumbly texture, it is ready to use as a mulch or soil additive.

If you plan to use the compost to make a growing substrate for your container plants, it is best to cover it with a tarp and let it mature for three months or longer. This will make sure that all composting processes have stopped and there will be no adverse affect on plant growth or germination when it is used.

ABOVE
Kitchen waste, such as fruit and vegetable scraps and eggshells, is generated everyday in most households and a great source of green material that is high in nitrogen.

LEFT
A simple wooden container is a great way of collecting your compost.

# Community Composting

It really pays to go to town when making compost. You will be removing a lot of fruit and vegetables at harvest time, which creates a nutrient gap that should be met by returning all the goodness back to the soil with as much aged compost as possible. Even in gardens with individual plots, there are still some real advantages to including a community composting area.

## Sourcing Organic Material

Some material will come from your own crop debris and waste, but this will not be enough on its own. The next step is to encourage members and plot renters to bring their own home vegetable and garden waste to the garden for composting. Although this requires some effort, it can be done, particularly where members are local to the garden. If they build it into their volunteering or vegetable-collection schedule, it is no extra effort, and it may even encourage them to work more often at the garden—needing to empty a compost container will be an added incentive to go in and do some weeding.

Befriend those working at local parks, gardeners, tree surgeons, and coffee houses to source free organic matter. Link your project up to other community organizations that might not be composting. You'll be helping them reduce their waste as well as getting more organic material. You could even offer a collection service and go around with a wheelbarrow or a trailer on the back of a bike.

Setting up a community composting site is also worth considering, but first check local legislation because the operation may need to be registered and inspected. On the plus side, it may help you attract volunteers and even some funding, because you will be helping local government reach their recycling targets. Composting locally also helps reduce transport miles.

## Composting Equipment

For a small compost pile made from garden and kitchen waste, you only need a garden fork to turn it occasionally. If people contribute garden clippings, then a shredding machine will be necessary. I would suggest that you initially stockpile the material and rent a shredder from time to time to process everything all at once. In community gardens with individual plots, you might consider having a shared area where renters can dump their woody clippings and then split the cost of renting equipment when needed.

LEFT
Make it easy for members to drop off their compost, or set up a community composting site for local residents, and you'll have a fine and continuous supply of fertility for your garden.

# Picking the Right Crop

It can be difficult to choose what to grow even if you're growing only on your own plot. If you garden is growing communally, it gets trickier to consider everyone's needs and wants. First, learn what your soil and climate are like and eliminate any crops that are not suitable for these conditions. Next, think about who you are growing for. Which crops do you or your members like?

Unless you are a small group that can decide collectively, delegate planning to the most experienced grower(s) in the first year, then you can make modifications as the plan begins to take shape. For example, if the seeds of one crop fail to germinate, it will provide an opportunity to fill in with an alternative.

## Efficient Use of Space

Space is at a premium in most community gardens. It will restrict the range of crops that can be grown, and there simply may not be room for some of the larger plants. However, by choosing varieties carefully and by making creative use of every surface, you will find that you have a lot more space than you think.

For example, training fruit trees as espaliers requires little space. It is also worth looking for bush varieties of some crops, such as sweet peppers or beans, that take up less room than some of the traditional types. A few crops, such as cauliflower, can be planted closer together to squeeze

more in, although you will get smaller heads as a result. Choose crops with multiple uses to make use of space; for example, peas can be initially harvested as sprouts for salads and then left to grow for the peas.

## Who's Picking?

For some community gardens, there might be a time of year when members are not around. Avoid plants whose main producing season falls at these times, and also steer clear of thirsty crops, such as courgette and lettuce, which will fail if there is nobody around to water them regularly. Concentrating your efforts on only the more productive seasons will allow you to build breaks into your seasonal calendar.

## Get the Perennials In

Plan early if you decide to grow any perennial vegetables or fruit. They often take two or more years to finish growing, and, if you delay, it can seem like an eternity to wait for the first harvest.

RIGHT
Training fruit trees, such as plums, to grow as espaliers can be highly productive and also help make the most of the space in your garden.

# Crop Rotation

Growing the same crop on the same piece of ground year after year can lead to nutrient deficiencies and a build up of pests and diseases. Instead, rotate crops around the plot. A good crop rotation will balance the feeding needs of different crops, break pest and disease cycles, and help control weeds. Designing a balanced rotation is an art, but some basic principles can help you get started.

There is no perfect rotation: it will depend on your site, the crops, and the gardener's inclinations. A community garden or individual plot can be split into many separate areas so that each is at a different stage of the rotation. In this manner, a varied range of crops is always available.

Crops are split into a number of different groups so that they fit different parts of the rotation. The main ones are brassicas (cabbage family), root crops (potatoes, parsnips), onion family (leeks and garlic), and legumes (peas and beans). Other categories might include salad crops, cucurbits, and grains, such as corn. Perennial crops cannot be included in a rotation.

## Root Structure

Spinach, lettuce, and onions, among others, have a shallow and spreading root system, while parsnips can go down many feet into the soil.

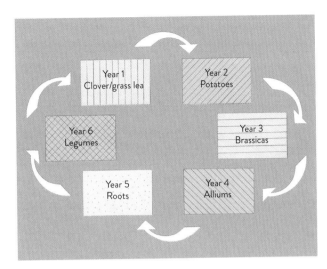

If possible, follow shallow rooters with deep rooters, because each of them will access nutrients from different parts of the soil.

## Leaf Form

Some plants are good at controlling weeds. Potatoes and squash, for example, smother almost everything underneath. Crops with thin or feathery, upright leaves, such as carrots and onions, however, are terrible at competing with weeds. If you grew only the latter type year after year on the same plot, your weeds would soon become unmanageable.

## What Nutrients?

Crops with a heavy nitrogen demand, such as brassicas and potatoes, are normally grown immediately after a fertility-building phase (see page 80). Less demanding crops, such as beans, tend to be planted toward the end of the rotation. Certain crops need more micronutrients than others. For example, brassicas need more boron than many other vegetables, so a three- or four-year gap between these crops will help prevent deficiencies. Even if space is too tight for you to leave areas uncropped, a long rotation and regular additions of well-rotted compost will help stop crops from exhausting certain nutrients.

## Building Fertility

Try to fit in a fertility-building phase, which will help your long-term soil condition. This usually comes close to the start of the cycle, and it is most usefully combined with a cover crop of green manure. This means that any available nutrients will be absorbed by the growing crop instead of being lost through leaching on bare soil. The fertility will then be available when you turn the cover crop and go on to plant your crop.

## Example of a Six-year Rotation Cycle

› **YEAR 1** Fertility building
› **YEAR 2** Spring—add rotted compost, plant potatoes
› **YEAR 3** Brassicas
› **YEAR 4** Add rotted compost and plant onions
› **YEAR 5** Carrots
› **YEAR 6** Peas—with a fertility building green manure cover crop sown in late summer or early autumn

**ABOVE**
The longer your rotation, the better. A four or six-year cycle is typical.

**LEFT**
Consider how your plant choices can be used to control weeds in your garden. For example, sprouts are heavy feeders that smother weeds. Carrots have deep tap roots and don't compete with weeds so well.

# Sowing Seeds

Most plants in your community garden will start their life as seeds. Buying good-quality seeds from reputable seed dealers, therefore, is vital, but having a good system for germinating and growing them will also help give your seedlings the best start. Some seeds need extra warmth to germinate, and seedlings of frost-tender plants may need weeks of protection before they are ready to go outdoors.

## Modules Versus Bare Root

Growing in seed module trays is a convenient way of raising plants from seeds, and it has become the "industry norm" for many crops. However, it does require a lot of plastic module trays (many of which are not strong or reusable), and it requires watering at least once a day or more in hot weather.

Bare-root transplants are seedlings that are grown directly in the soil from seeds and then dug up and transplanted to their final location. These transplants are cheaper because no trays or potting compost are required, and if there is a delay with ground preparation, bare-root transplants will cope much better. Plants left too long in their trays will get rootbound and suffer.

Bare-root systems work particularly well for brassicas and leeks, yet there are plenty of crops that can be sown directly into the soil. Some crops cannot be transplanted, such as carrots and parsnips, so sow these directly in their final growing space.

## Heating

In most climates, heated facilities are useful if not essential for part of the year, and you might want to construct a hardening-off area (see facing page) to ease your transplants from their cosseted beginnings into the open field. However, the cost of extra heat will increase your expenditure.

Heat-loving crops, such as sweet peppers and tomatoes, need a long growing season and temperatures of at least 21°C (70°F) for good germination. Heated benches are the cheapest way to achieve this, using cables buried in sand or store-bought heated mats, particularly if you make a specially insulated area in your greenhouse to keep the heat in.

## Hardening Off

Even frost-hardy crops, such as cabbage, resent the shock of coming from a warm greenhouse into the cold open air. Acclimatizing them to their new environment is called hardening off, and, on a small scale, it can be done by bringing the seedlings outside during the day and back in at night.

If there are a lot of plants, however, this is time-consuming, so the alternative is to have an unheated tunnel, preferably with some side ventilation, that the young plants can sit in for a week or so before being planted out in the open.

## Buying Or Raising?

Most growers instinctively want to raise their own plants. However, it is deceptively expensive. Try counting up the time spent sowing, ventilating, and watering, as well as the energy cost of heating. You may find it is much cheaper to buy plants from a nursery or garden centre than propagating your own.

**ABOVE**
Sowing seeds directly into the soil is straightforward and cheap, but it does not suit all crops. Already-grown plants can be established more quickly.

# Saving Seeds

It is not necessary to save seeds to have a successful community garden. I find that saving at least some of your own seeds, however, brings a completeness to growing because you are involved in every part of the life cycle. It is also a great way of involving community members and linking with your garden's other plot renters or other gardeners in your neighbourhood (see page 56).

It is possible to develop strains or even new varieties of crops that are particularly suited to your garden and its microclimate. They might also become more resistant to local strains of pests or diseases as time goes on. You will not be able to save all your own seeds to begin with (or perhaps even at all), so try a couple of easy ones to start with, such as beans.

## Open-Pollinated Seeds

Seed that comes from open-pollinated varieties will not be labelled as F1. It is important to know the difference if you are saving seeds, because seeds from F1 hybrids will not come true; in other words, the next generation will not be the same as the parents you took the seeds from. For this reason, if you want to save seeds, use only open-pollinated varieties.

## Pollination

Understand how your chosen vegetable pollinates. Some, such as tomatoes, are almost predominantly self-pollinating due to the structure of the flower, while others, such as brassicas, cross readily with a range of similar plants. For example, kale, cauliflower, and cabbages all interbreed.

Corn is pollinated by wind, so it can be pollinated by plants miles away from your garden. Squash plants have separate male and female flowers, while others have both male and female parts in the same flower.

Where crossbreeding can occur, you might want to control the seeds that will result by isolating the plants. You can do this by screening off one crop from another during flowering, or by growing one variety at a different time than

the others. Alternatively, you could just let nature take its course and see what results.

Cross-pollination is a much bigger issue for community gardens with multiple individual plots because there is usually a much wider range of varieties grown. With care, however, each gardener can still save his or her own seeds.

## Labelling

Labelling your plants is an important part of good seed-saving, yet it is all too easily overlooked. From early in the growing season, identify the plants from which seeds are to be kept and tie a label to those plants with something fairly permanent. This is particularly sensible in communal gardens where there is a good chance of a volunteer picking your chosen seed beans to put in the lunch pot.

## How Many Plants?

Although it varies from plant to plant, it is generally recommended that you grow at least thirty plants of any variety to be sure you have a wide enough gene pool. For some crops, this is easy—for example, carrots and leeks, which take up hardly any space. For crops such as tomatoes, it might be more difficult.

Try cooperating with other gardening groups and sharing seeds collectively. One garden could save bean seeds, for example, and another could save lettuce seeds; you can then exchange seeds each year. This cuts down on the work for each garden and spreads the risk if one grower has a disaster. Community gardens can also set up garden-wide seed-saving and -sharing days for individual plot holders.

LEFT
When deciding which seeds to save, it is important to consider the plant's health, vigour, and taste as well as appearance.

# Flowers for Pest Control

Flowers don't just look pretty and taste good, they are also helpful in the struggle to keep pest populations under control. They attract predators, distract and deter pests with their scent, and break up the monochrome of single crops by making them more dispersed and, therefore, harder for pests to find. The greater the flower diversity, the better—especially if they have multiple uses.

## Encouraging Predators

Perhaps the most important tool against pests is a balanced ecosystem. A garden is by nature a man-made construction, but the greater the diversity of plants at different stages of development during the year, the better it is. It is no good expecting pest predators to be in your garden ready to eat a particular critter if you haven't provided food for the predators all year round or an overwintering habitat for them.

If a specific pest is a problem, research what will eat it and what they need. It might be beetles, birds, or other predatory insects. Keep in mind that it will be necessary to tolerate low levels of the pest to give these natural predators a constant food supply.

Creating special habitats with a range of flowering plants can make a significant impact. For example, beetles are one of the main slug predators, so design a beetle bank with a range of flowering grasses that form tussocks as well as flowers that are pollinated by beetles, such as *Solidago* and *Spiraea*.

## Deterrents

Herbs, being highly scented, are great for confusing and deterring pests. If it smells a little pungent or bitter, the chances are that pests will not like it. All members of the onion family have this ability hence the range of garlic products available to buy. Coriander, basil, and oregano—among others—will all help to keep pests away from crops, as will anything with a lemon scent, such as lemon balm, lemon thyme, or lemongrass.

## Letting Crops Flower

If you are a "tidy" gardener, you will probably want to clear out a plant as soon as you have harvested from it and get ready for the next one. However, a degree of chaos is actually good for a garden. Leaving some of your crop

your crop plants will help with pest and disease control both above and below ground.

For example, I always let a few of my brassica plants flower because they provide food for the parasitic wasps that eat cabbage white butterflies, or imported cabbageworm. Similarly, many mycorrhizal fungi require their associate plant to go through its entire life cycle so it can multiply; if we remove the plant before it has flowered and seeded, we will be reducing diversity underground, too.

## Distraction

Many pests, most notably the carrot fly maggot, find their food by scent, so mixing up crops and planting highly scented plants around the edge of them helps to camouflage the plants you want to protect. For those pests that locate food by sight, a similar distraction can be created by scattering flowers or herbs among the crop. It won't be possible to keep all the pests away, but you can reduce pest populations and give the predators a chance to control them.

**ABOVE**
Parsley flowers have flower heads that not only add a splash of light colour to the garden but also attract soldier beetles and other insect pollinators.

# Task List:
# Spring/Early Summer

Things happen so quickly once spring starts that it can be hard to keep in mind everything that needs to be done. Getting a week or two behind, particularly with sowing and planting schedules, can really throw off production later in the season, so it is essential to plan all your different spring and early summer tasks.

## Create a Schedule

However experienced you are, I recommend creating a sowing and planting schedule. Include in it the dates on which to begin soil preparation in plenty of time for each successional sowing.

## Ground Preparation

You will probably have done some soil preparation during the previous autumn or winter. However, if you have a good cover crop sown to protect the soil over winter, you will need to cut it back and dig it into the soil in good time. Most plants (particularly rye grasses) release chemicals as they decompose that stop seeds from germinating. Give at least four to six weeks before you sow seeds directly into the soil. Sowing into trays and transplanting can shorten this interval.

I often fertilize my soil in the spring, adding well-aged compost or manure to the cover crop part of my rotation.

## Sowing Seeds

Some crops need a really early start. Sweet peppers and onions, for example, like a long season, so they should be sown a month or two before most of your other seeds. Consider heated propagation for an early start, and make sure you have the facility to keep seedlings growing well under cover before it is time to move them outside. At this time, they will also need to be hardened off (see pages 92–93).

## Planting

Sowing seeds directly where they are to grow is certainly the cheapest and most straightforward way to grow crops, but it doesn't always work. You may have problems with slugs or mice, a cold wet climate, or trouble with competing weeds. Sowing seeds first into seed trays gives you more control over temperature and moisture and allows the plant to become more established. In theory, the seedling then competes better against weeds and pests once planted outside.

## Start Weeding

Spring and early summer is also a crucial weeding time. Later in the season, crops may be able to cope with some competition, but in their seedling stage, keeping them weed-free is essential if they are to get the light and water they need to thrive.

Keeping up with the weeds, particularly in warm and wet springs, is always a challenge. There is an old saying that if you can see the weeds, it's too late. While that may be extreme, little and often is definitely the key.

One lesson I learned early on in my professional career is always to start a weeding session on your cleanest bed. This seems counterintuitive, but it takes only seconds to run a hoe over a bed of tiny weed seedlings, and it means that bed is always clean. Afterward, you can then go on to tackle the worst offenders.

**LEFT**
Planting is a great job for your whole group to get involved with. As well as being more social and fun, it can make the job shorter, saving everyone's backs.

# Task List: Late Summer and Autumn

When summer starts to recede and autumn spreads its blanket over the ground, jobs become less urgent. However, there are still some that need to be done within a definite time frame. Fruit still needs picking, particularly soft fruit such as raspberries, which will need a regular harvest to prevent them from spoiling. If you use cover crops, sow them in plenty of time before it gets too cold.

Some tasks come under the category of "do them now and they're easy; leave them until spring and they're not." Some forward thinking and planning at the end of the year can save you time and heartache once the chaos of the new season starts.

## Ground Preparation

I am a big believer in keeping soil covered, if possible by something living, although I also use cardboard and organic mulches. If you are mulching, autumn is a good time to cut back any growth from previous crops. Leave this debris on the surface and cover with plain cardboard or straw. This blocks out light and allows loose nutrients to be absorbed for later release. You can also add a thick layer of garden compost or well-rotted manure. The plant residues will die over the winter and hopefully give you easy-to-work soil the following spring.

## Sowing and Planting

Late summer and early autumn is a good time to get a cover crop sown, when the preceding crop has finished, but don't forget those crops that like being out over winter, such as garlic, shallots, and broad beans, which can all be planted in the autumn.

Cover crops are useful over winter because they are great at mopping up any loose nutrients in the soil that might be otherwise lost to winter rains. They also protect the structure of the soil and add valuable organic matter to the ground when you dig them back in. For late sowing, try rye grasses or quick-maturing crops, such as mustard and phacelia.

## Saving Seeds

Some plants will seed in late summer, but most come in to their own in autumn. Collect from open-pollinated varieties (see page 95) and make sure you harvest the seeds as dry as possible; you will probably need to dry them further in either a dry shed or warm room. Once dry, store them in a cool, dry place.

## Looking Ahead to Winter

Winter evenings are a time for planning and drawing up the rotations for next year.

In mild climates, winter is also a great time for giving fruit trees a formative prune, except for cherries, plums, and other stone fruits, which need to be done in summer. Avoid pruning if a hard frost is forecast because the cold can cause damage to fresh wounds.

**ABOVE**
Autumn to early winter is one of the best times of year to dig and turn over the soil, aerating the ground before it becomes too wet and freezes.

## Chapter 4

# PLANT DIRECTORY

This final chapter is a snapshot of some of my favourite fruits, herbs, and vegetables. Along with general growing advice, I've included some tips picked up along the years from either my own experiences or from the many amazing growers I meet as part of my job. Although some crops are more difficult to grow than others, if you want to grow a particular one, then it is worth trying. You might have a knack with salad greens, or you might have more success growing fruit. If you're lucky, within your gardening community will be a full range of abilities and skills for most crops. I try not to be prescriptive, because there is always more than one way of growing and, with the effects of climate change increasing, some of the gardening "rules" that you read about in books can be taken with a pinch of salt. So experiment and have fun.

# Asparagus

In the right conditions, asparagus can grow like a weed, but it comes at a time when you're hungry for fresh greens. I could gladly eat it every day for the six weeks or so it is in season.

**LIFESPAN**
Long-lived perennial

**PLANT**
One-year-old crowns about four weeks before the last expected spring frost

**GROW IN**
Light, well-drained soil; it hates having wet feet

## Planting Tips

Set the crowns on a ridge at a depth of 5 cm (2 inches). This will help with drainage during the winter. Gently spread out the "fingers" of the roots as if they were an outstretched hand and backfill with soil so that the bud tips are just covered.

## Cultivation

Asparagus plants need at least three years to become established. In this time, do not harvest the shoots and remove weeds as they appear. Support the ferny growth with stakes and twine, and cut it all back in late autumn. Feed with a general fertilizer in early spring and again after harvest.

## Weed Control

Keeping asparagus weed-free is the biggest challenge, because it has thin foliage that doesn't compete well.

Mulching regularly with weed-free aged compost or mulch reduces weeds as well as making their removal easier. Some growers cover the crowns with cardboard after cutting back the foliage. They then remove this covering in spring when the first spears start pushing up.

## Harvest

Only harvest the thick spears from at least three-year-old plants in late spring and early summer. Cut just below the surface with a sharp knife.

## Container Tips

You can grow asparagus in containers—just make sure you have one that is big and deep because asparagus roots grow to quite a depth. Also keep in mind you have to wait several years before you can harvest the spears, so you will have to be patient with watering and care before the reward.

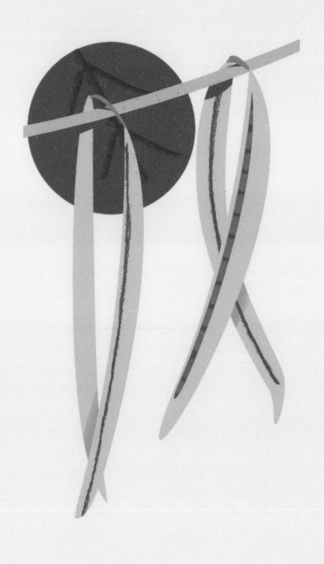

# Green Beans

These are one of those vegetables that are much better served as fresh as possible. They're easy to grow, and climbing pole plants can go on producing for many weeks, making them cheaper as well as tastier than buying at the store.

LIFESPAN
Annual

**PLANT**
Sow seeds directly into the soil after the danger of frost passes; make succession sowings for bush beans; in mild-winter areas, sow pole beans again in late summer for an autumn harvest

GROW IN
Well-drained, fertile soil

## Planting Tips

For climbing pole beans, you can start sowing seeds once the soil reaches a temperature of 18–24°C (65–70°F); for bush beans, you can start sowing when it's 15.5°C (60°F). Sow bush bean seeds every two weeks to ensure a steady supply of beans.

## Cultivation

Provide a sturdy support for climbing pole beans to twine around. Bush green beans are easier, because they don't need anything to climb up, but you do have to bend down to pick them and they don't crop for as long. Be sure to provide regular irrigation for consistent cropping.

## Weed Control

Pay attention to weeding in the initial stages of growth and cover the soil with a mulch. Climbing pole beans can be undercropped with ground-cover plants, such as trailing squashes—but ensure there is room to stand and pick, or a low growing cover crop like yellow trefoil.

## Harvest

Pick regularly, particularly when the weather is wet, because the beans are best young and will quickly become large and tough to eat. Leave a few on the plant at the end of the season to mature, and then pick and dry, either to sow next year or to use as a dried bean over the winter.

## Container Tips

Keep the plants well fed and watered when growing in containers. Pole beans are ideal for growing up a trellis or fence, especially in full sun.

# Beetroot

Beetroots are a versatile crop and relatively easy to grow. You can grow them well in either soil or in a container and harvest them small or large. If you choose the right cultivar, they can stand some frost, too.

**LIFESPAN**
Biennial

**PLANT**
Can be sown any time from spring to early autumn

**GROW IN**
Fertile, well-drained soil in the open ground or in containers

## Planting Tips

Some beetroot seeds contain two or three small seeds, so sow thinly to take account of this.

## Cultivation

Choose a sunny site and provide plenty of water early on when the root starts to swell, about eight weeks after sowing. In hot conditions, they tend to go to seed (bolt); regular but not excessive watering helps to prevent this.

## Weed control

Beetroot crops are reasonably tolerant of weeds, but it is important to do at least one hand weed at the seedling stage. After that, using a hoe is the quickest way, but be careful to avoid damaging the roots.

## Harvest

You can thin the crop and harvest baby beetroot at the same time. Leave the other roots to continue developing, and harvest when they are about 5 cm (2 inches) in diameter.

## Container Tips

Space in containers is precious, so what you can do is sow thickly and then harvest the majority as baby salad greens or baby beetroot. Leave a few of the strongest seedlings to grow into mature beetroot.

# Florence Fennel

The "bulbs" of this plant are crisp with a liquorice flavour when raw and with a sweet, deep flavour when slowly braised. It can be a little difficult to grow, particularly because it is not always easy to prevent it from going to seed, but it is well worth the effort in my mind.

**LIFESPAN**
Annual

**PLANT**
Sow seeds in spring after danger of frost passes or in late summer for an autumn crop

**GROW IN**
Free-draining, fertile soil with plenty of water and loads of sun

## Planting Tips

Fennel can be sown closely and harvested when young, at which stage you can eat the whole plant. Alternatively, sow in seed flats divided into compartments and transplant the seedlings, but be careful to avoid damaging the baby roots when doing this and provide plenty of water when the seedlings are in their new locations.

## Cultivation

While fennel needs plenty of water during growth, root rot can occur if the soil remains too wet. Once the stems begin to swell at the bases, draw soil up around them to blanch them, making the "bulbs" paler and sweeter.

## Weed Control

Keep the plants free of weeds with regular hand weeding and hoeing.

A layer of mulch will help suppress weeds and keep moisture in the soil.

## Harvest

You can harvest at any time. When the bulb is completely mature, the stem can get tough to eat, although it is still good added to stocks or broths. If the plants do go to seed, harvest and eat the seeds, too.

## Container Tip

Growing herb or bronze fennel in pots gives a constant supply of the aniseed flavour for a long season.

# Carrots

Easy to grow, although not necessarily easy to grow well, carrots are a staple of most vegetable plots and community gardens. Quick-maturing cultivars can produce early crops, especially if grown under cover, while later cultivars, stored well, can last through much of the winter.

**LIFESPAN**
Biennial

**PLANT**
Sow directly into soil or containers from spring onward but not when temperature goes above 29°C (85°F)

**GROW IN**
Best in a light, sandy soil, but adequate crops can be grown in most situations

## Planting Tips

To an extent, sowing density depends on cultivar, soil type, and how big you want your carrots. I sow a little more than I need and thin to the desired spacing, although this can attract pests by bruising the leaves and releasing the carrot smell.

## Cultivation

Small numbers of seeds can be sown every few weeks to avoid a bumper crop later in the season and to ensure continuity of supply. While it is useful to water carrots during dry spells, they should not be overwatered. If you can, leave a few plants to go to seed, because carrot flowers and seeds are particularly good for attracting beneficial insects.

## Weed Control

Carrots need a lot of weeding to avoid being swamped, especially in wet years. Try this trick to give you a head start:

› Sow the seeds and then cover the end of the row with a sheet of clear plastic. The weeds under the plastic will germinate a little quicker.
› As soon as you see weeds showing under the plastic, go over the whole row with a weed burner or hand weed. This will kill all weeds that have germinated in the rest of the row but that are not yet showing. The carrots themselves will not be harmed, because they germinate a little slower.

## Harvest

The roots can be harvested at any size, although they are awkward to handle when small. Roots left in the ground too long may experience pest damage. You can also eat the foliage, which can be added to soups and stews. The seeds are also edible.

## Container Tips

Carrots do well in containers. Try to find short, early, or quick-maturing cultivars and water well.

# Chard

Being related to spinach and beetroot, this leafy green vegetable is also known as "spinach beet." It is hardier and higher yielding than true spinach, and less prone to going to seed early (bolting). It has a slightly stronger flavour, which is not to everyone's taste, but it is one that I love.

LIFESPAN
Biennial

PLANT
Sow directly in soil or in seed flats, from spring to summer, and in mild-summer areas again in autumn

GROW IN
Most rich soil in sun is suitable; will grow in light shade

## Planting Tips

The seed germinates easily and can be sown directly into the final position or in seed flats for transplanting. I often sow thickly to allow for slug damage and then thin to an end spacing of 10–20 cm (4–8 inches) between plants. The thinned leaves can be eaten.

## Cultivation

Chard is hardy—especially the white variety. It will keep growing even in relatively low temperatures. Plants sown late in the summer might overwinter in mild-winter areas and give a good early crop in the late spring and early summer. They are originally maritime plants, so they grow particularly well in seaside locations.

## Weed Control

Chard is vigorous and competes well with weeds, although at the seedling stage the emerging crop will need some hand weeding.

## Harvest

You can harvest the leaves of chard in a number of ways:

› Remove the outer leaves by pulling down and out (like you do rhubarb), leaving the leaves in the centre to continue growing.
› Cut the whole plant down and let it regrow. Be careful not to cut into the growing centre.
› Pull up the entire plant, leaving the ground free for something else.

You can eat the leaf stems too. Slice them thinly and sauté with some onion and red wine.

## Container Tip

If you choose the ruby or rainbow mixes, chard is a stunning plant that can double as an ornamental (and secretly productive) pot plant.

# Courgette

Courgette plants are easy-to-grow, summer-producing annuals that yield up to a dozen succulent courgettes (sometimes called "zucchini") during the summer months—ideal for community gardens, where the bounty can be readily shared. I particularly like the "Striato di Napoli" variety.

**LIFESPAN**
Annual

**PLANT**
Sow two weeks before the last frost in seed flats, or straight into the soil when it reaches 15.5°C (60°F) in spring

**GROW IN**
Well-drained, fertile soil in full sun

## Planting Tips

I usually sow a couple of seeds into a small pot. If both germinate, I pinch the weaker one and transplant the strong plant once a couple of leaves reach a good size. If the soil is well drained and warm, you can sow directly into the soil. Plant only after the risk of frost has passed.

## Cultivation

Courgettes are usually vigorous and pest free, although seedlings are vulnerable to low night temperatures and hungry slugs and snails. Powdery mildew can be a problem later in the season, and if it gets too bad, you will just have to consign the plant to the compost pile. In dry conditions, water well to make sure of a good succession of fruit.

## Weed Control

Weeds are not usually a big issue, because courgettes grow quickly with large, dense leaves. A good way to be sure that you never need to weed is to use a mulch of biodegradable plastic; by the time it starts to degrade, your plant will be smothering any weeds. Alternatively, you can plant into a cover crop of vetch—just clear an 80-cm² (12-square-inch) area and keep it clear until the courgette plant is big enough to fend for itself.

## Harvest

I like picking courgettes small and sautéing or grilling them either whole or sliced in two lengthwise. You will need to pick regularly to avoid them getting too big, especially if the weather is warm and wet and they produce prolifically. Pick the courgettes young with the flower intact for stuffed courgette flowers. If you are looking for income from your community garden, these can also be a good cash crop for selling to high-end restaurants.

## Container Tips

The plants will need a big pot and fertile soil mix. Water at least once a day, or more in hot weather.

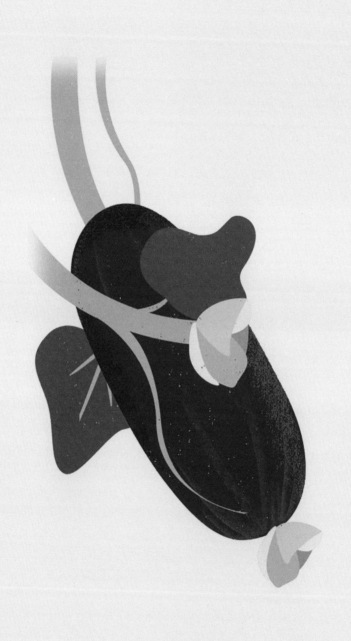

# Cucumber

Cucumbers are perfect for summer salads, gazpacho, and yogurt-based dips. Although they need a lot of water, they are perfect for most community gardens, and if you choose the right cultivar, they can grow well outside, either trained or left to scramble.

**LIFESPAN**
Annual

**PLANT**
Raise seeds only indoors; a temperature of 15–29°C (60  85°F) is required for germination—even if sowing an outdoor variety

**GROW IN**
Well-drained, fertile soil in full sun

## Planting Tips

Be sure the seedlings are well protected, because they hate wind and cold, and only plant outside once the risk of frost has passed. In heavy soil, avoid overwatering when the plants are young. Once the plants start to grow, overwatering becomes less of a risk.

## Cultivation

Cucumbers like high humidity and warm weather. They especially like warm nights. If possible, grow them separated from tomatoes, which prefer it much drier. You can spray the leaves with water a couple of times a day or keep the paths wet if growing in a tunnel or greenhouse but they will grow happily outdoors in hotter areas.

## Weed Control

I often cover the soil with a layer of cardboard to keep the root zone moist and reduce weed competition.

## Harvest

Wait until the whole cucumber has thickened up, particularly if growing long cultivars. A healthy, productive plant should produce a cucumber every couple of days. Make sure you pick before it becomes yellow and watery. You can also pick them small for pickling, although there are cultivars specifically bred for this purpose. The flowers are edible and are sometimes added to salads.

## Container Tip

Choose one of the outdoor-type ridge cultivars, which you can grow in a container outdoors with or without a support. Unsupported, they will scramble over the edge, and you can just pull the vine back up if it gets in the way.

# Garlic

I can't imagine cooking without the alliums: onions, leeks, and garlic are all in this botanical genus. Garlic keeps well through the winter but can also be harvested fresh (or "wet") in the early summer.

**LIFESPAN**
Biennial

**PLANT**
Sink cloves into soil in autumn, four to six weeks before first frost

**GROW IN**
Tolerant of most soils, with a preference for those that are light and that drain freely

## Planting Tips

Separate the bulb into individual cloves, then push each clove into the soil at a depth of 2.5–5 cm (1–2 inches) with the pointed shoot end directed upward. Ideally, they should be about 15 cm (6 inches) apart in rows 50 cm (20 inches) apart.

## Cultivation

Garlic is straightforward to grow but it is not always easy to get a bulb of a decent size. Choosing the best variety is important, as is watering the plants as they develop in late spring.

## Weed Control

Don't worry about keeping the garlic bed weeded over the winter; a few weeds will help protect the soil and disguise your crop from pests. Once spring starts and the bulbs begin to grow, keep the area weeded to let them develop and allow air to circulate.

## Harvest

Either harvest fresh as soon as the bulbs have formed in late spring to summer, depending where you live, or wait until the leaves start to die. Unlike onions, it is best not to wait until all the leaves are brown, because the bulbs may split and not keep for as long. Dry the bulbs in the sun if they will be stored.

## Container Tip

Garlic is great for containers, because it likes well-drained soil and has shallow roots. Plant it on its own, or around the base of taller plants. For instance, leave a space in the middle of a circle of garlic and then plant climbing green beans.

# Leeks

Similar to garlic, leeks provide a fresh harvest at times of famine. Hardy cultivars keep going through the winter, ready for harvest at any time and into spring. They're also relatively free of pests and diseases, so they are good for gardeners at all skill levels.

**LIFESPAN**
Biennial

**PLANT**
Sow in flats 10–12 weeks before moving outdoors; in mild-summer or cold-winter areas, transplant in spring; in other areas, do so in late summer and autumn

**GROW IN**
Most soils are suitable, even those that are fairly heavy

## Planting Tips

When the seedlings are about 20 cm (8 inches) tall, use a dibble (or thick pointed stick) to make a deep hole 10–15 cm (4–6 inches) in the ground and drop the seedling into it. You may need to trim the roots if they are tangled. The deeper you dig, the longer the white shaft and most tender part of the leek will be.

## Cultivation

Drawing soil up around the stems of the leeks as they grow is not essential, but it is a way of controlling weeds and increasing the length of the white shaft. You can add a dressing of high-nitrogen fertilizer in late summer.

## Weed control

I tend to hoe leeks regularly early in the season, when they are most vulnerable, and once they are a good size, I leave the weeds to their own devices. Although this can make harvesting difficult in a warm winter, when the weeds keep growing, it does protect the soil and provide a habitat for wildlife.

## Harvest

Leeks can be harvested at any stage, from pencil thickness (a favourite of one chef that I used to supply) right up to 5 cm thick for some cultivars. Left too late, however, the flower head will begin to form and the leeks will be unusable. The specific time of harvest will depend on cultivar and season, but, with careful planning, you should be able to have leeks in production almost all year round.

## Container Tip

In containers, leeks need more moisture than garlic and can go to seed if not kept well watered.

# Kale

Finding fame again recently as one of
the new breed of superfoods, kale is
a must for almost any vegetable plot.
Easy to grow and productive at most
times of year, you can eat it as baby
leaf in salads or as a large-leafed green.

**LIFESPAN**
Biennial

**PLANT**
Sow in midsummer for an
autumn crop; in mild-summer
areas, plant in spring and in
midsummer for an autumn
crop; in hot-summer areas,
plant outside in late summer

**GROW IN**
Most soil with high fertility
is suitable

## Planting Tips

Sow seeds in flats or start from
transplants. Transplants can be planted
in dense rows, then later moved to
their final planting position. Because
kale, like all plants in the cabbage
family (brassicas), does well in cool
climates, the seeds will germinate at
temperatures as low as 4°C (40°F). In
mild-winter areas, plant kale only in
summer; in these areas, you can try
growing collards in the same way, but
sowing seeds outdoors in autumn for
an early spring crop.

## Cultivation

Water well after planting, but water
sparingly once the seedlings are
established. All cultivars are hardy
and most will withstand long periods
below freezing and snow. You can
undersow with a low-growing cover
crop of legume seeds, such as white
clover, when the plants are a few
inches tall to protect the soil. To
protect from common pests, such as
birds and caterpillars, cover the crop
with netting.

## Weed Control

A couple of weeding sessions in the
early stages of growth is normally
enough to keep plants weed free,
particularly if you planted them close
together. Brassicas have dense foliage
and are said to have an allelopathic
effect, whereby chemicals exuded
through their roots can inhibit the
germination of weeds nearby.

## Harvest

Unless harvesting as a salad green, wait
until the plant is a good size before
picking. Pick too early and you will
hinder the plant's development and
reduce overall yield. Remove individual
leaves as required.

## Container Tip

Brassicas generally don't do that well
in containers. This is because they need
plenty of fertility and moisture. Kale,
however, is worth trying, particularly
one of the less vigorous cultivars, such
as "Cavolo Nero."

# 'Purple Sprouting' Broccoli

'Purple Sprouting' broccoli is similar to baby broccoli (or Broccolini) in having a small head but numerous side shoots—harvesting the shoots encourages more growth.

**LIFESPAN**
Biennial

**PLANT**
Sow in mid-spring for transplanting in early summer and again in early summer for transplanting in late summer

**GROW IN**
Rich, well-drained soil

## Planting Tips

With unpredictable winters in many parts of the world, it is becoming increasingly difficult to plan accurately. Choose 'Purple Sprouting', 'White Sprouting', or another variety of heading broccoli to suit the conditions in your area. If you follow the guidelines for the cultivar you choose, you should get a good crop—even if it is not at the exact time you planned.

## Cultivation

Water well after planting and during dry spells; otherwise, water sparingly. In winter, you may need to support the plants with stakes to prevent them from being blown over. To protect them from common pests, such as birds and caterpillars, cover the crop with netting.

## Weed Control

As with kale, a couple of weeding sessions in the early stages of growth is normally enough to keep the plants free of weeds.

## Harvest

Start picking as soon as the flower shoots sprout. For cultivars that have a larger head in the centre, you may need to harvest the head to encourage the side shoots to develop. Keep picking for as long as you can. With plants in the cabbage family (brassicas), you can eat pretty much every part of the plant so don't stop once the yellow flowers open. As long as the flower stalk is still tender, you can keep harvesting for a long time.

## Container Tip

'Purple Sprouting' broccoli is not recommended for growing in anything but the largest container.

# Salad Greens

What we refer to as "salad greens" covers a wide range of plant families and seasons, but I will mainly focus on lettuce and brassicas. They can be grown almost anywhere, even in pots on the windowsill, and at any time of year. Add some bitter greens, and you'll have mesclun.

**LIFESPAN**
Annual

**PLANT**
Almost all year round, depending on variety

**GROW IN**
Most soil can be used to grow salad greens, but fertile, well-drained soil is best

## Planting Tips

Most salad green varieties germinate easily, although lettuce doesn't like hot temperatures, so try sowing in the evening in light shade to prevent it from becoming dormant, and avoid sowing in summer in hot-summer areas. The real trick with these greens is to get a continuous crop. Make a succession of sowings of a small number of different varieties every few weeks, starting in early spring and carrying on through late autumn. In warm climates, you can sow brassicas throughout the year. Sow their seeds into flats for later transplanting or directly where they are to grow. It partly depends on how you intend to harvest. For cut-and-come-again crops, a thick sowing can work well to smother weeds, but if you want whole heads of lettuce, I would recommend transplanting or thinning plants to their final spacing. The thinnings, of course, can be eaten.

## Cultivation

You will need to keep salad greens well watered. If they dry out, they will quickly go to seed (bolt). Always water after harvest because they will

be stressed from being disturbed; the secondary stress of no water can cause premature bolting. Short-lived salad greens will need little in the way of supplementary feeding. They grow best at a temperature range of 10–20°C (50–68°F); salad greens that tend to bolt easily during high summer temperatures are best grown during the cooler months of spring or autumn or grown in a cool area in light shade. The use of floating row covers will help sustain crops during the cooler months.

## Weed Control

As long as the site is relatively free of weeds on sowing or planting, weeding is not normally difficult because salad greens tend to grow quickly. After initial weeding or hoeing, they will outcompete most weeds. The exceptions are some of the feathery leaved Asian brassicas, such as mizuna.

## Harvest

A good harvesting plan can almost double your crop of salad greens. Broadly speaking, there are three different ways of harvesting:

- Leave the whole head to develop and then harvest it all at once by cutting it at the base. If you don't cut too low, some cultivars will produce a second or even third crop, but they will be much smaller.
- Sow thickly and harvest as small leaves on a cut-and-come-again basis. Depending on the weather and how hard you cut them back, you might get up to five or six decent crops. Look out for loose-leaf lettuce cultivars, such as 'Lollo Rossa' and oak-leaf types. Asian brassicas also suit this method.
- You can pick the outer leaves from each plant as they reach a suitable size. This is more time-consuming but has distinct advantages: it make the plants last longer, it provides a greater harvest, and by raising the crown of the plant and never having old leaves, you increase airflow and reduce disease.

## Container Tip

Sow those varieties more suited to hot, dry climates, such as amaranth and basil, although with enough watering, almost all salad greens will do well in pots.

**Plants you can grow as salad greens:**
- Lettuce
- Some herbs, including basil, coriander, parsley, and fennel
- Mustards and Asian brassicas, such as mizuna and bok choy
- Leafy vegetable greens, such as kale, Swiss chard, and carrot and beetroot leaves
- Pea shoots and leaves
- "Weeds," such as dandelion, chicory, and sorrel are great at the cooler ends of the season and in small quantities. They will become bitter and tough, however, when the weather is hot.

# Peas

Peas are the perfect crop for a
community garden. They are easy to grow
and are best picked and eaten straight
from the vine. I rarely get any peas home,
because my kids go crazy for them when
they come to "help" in our garden.

**LIFESPAN**
Annual

**PLANT**
Sow mostly in spring and
autumn or winter; in mild-
summer areas, also through
the summer

**GROW IN**
Most well-drained soil is
suitable; they don't need
high fertility

## Planting Tips

Peas germinate easily, so unless
you have a problem with mice or
other small rodents in your plot, I
recommend sowing directly into the
soil 2 cm (1 inch) or so deep. If growing
for pea shoots in salad, you can sow
thickly; otherwise, space out to 5 cm
(1-2 inches) apart.

## Cultivation

There are some modern dwarf plants
that manage with little support. For
small areas, however, I prefer the
taller types that produce over a long
period of time. Train them up stakes
or trellises and water well, especially
at flowering time and when the pods
begin to swell.

## Weed Control

Keep the plants well weeded, especially
in the initial stages. Once they start
climbing they can cope with some
weed competition. Try undersowing
with a cover crop of clover.

## Harvest

I love pea shoots in salad; just pinch
them off between your thumb and
index finger. If harvesting for sugar
snap or snow peas, pick the pods
regularly when they are young, or
they can get stringy. For garden peas,
harvest once the pods have swelled; if
left too long, the pods will start to dry
out and the peas inside will be tough.

## Container Tip

Peas can grow well in containers, but
they will need sufficient watering,
particularly once the pods develop.

# Potatoes

Growing potatoes is easy and loads of fun. Burrowing through the soil to find the tubers is like looking for buried treasure. They do take up a lot of space, however, so I normally grow only early potatoes that are in the ground for less time than a main crop of potatoes.

**LIFESPAN**
Annual

**PLANT**
Bury seed potatoes three to four weeks before last spring frost; in hot-summer areas, again in late summer or autumn

**GROW IN**
Any rich and fertile, well-drained soil

## Planting Tips

Potatoes prefer plenty of sun, and they are heavy feeders, so either plant after your fertility-building phase of rotation or add well-rotted compost and manure before planting.

You'll be planting "seed" potatoes, which look like normal potatoes, but they have eyes and come from a specialty garden centre certified free of disease. For an earlier crop, place the seed potatoes on a tray lined with newspaper and put somewhere to dry and to let the eyes shoot. When the shoots are 2 cm (1 inch) long, the potatoes are ready to be planted 8–15 cm (3–6 inches) deep, in rows 50–75 cm (20–30 inches) apart.

## Cultivation

The young shoots of early crops may need protecting from night frost with a floating row cover, which can be removed once the weather warms up. Unless the weather is dry, you shouldn't need to water until new tubers start to form, which is usually about the same time that the plants begin to flower. Potato tubers exposed to light will turn green and become poisonous. To prevent this, take some of the soil from between the rows and hill it up in a ridge over the emerging shoots to cover the tubers. There are a few pests and diseases to watch out for: late summer blight is the worst, and it can be avoided by growing only early cultivars that are harvested before blight can take hold.

## Weed Control

Potatoes are great at smothering weeds, but they do take time to get going. The traditional process of hilling them is also a good way of keeping them weeded at an early stage, and it helps to warm up the soil on the ridge.

## Harvest

When the leaves begin to die down, or soon after flowers appear, your potatoes are ready to harvest. Keep later cultivars intended for storing in the ground for a few weeks so that the skin hardens. Scrape the skin lightly with your nail to test; if you don't leave a mark, they are ready to dig. Early cultivars are not suitable for storing.

## Container Tip

Choose a container at least 60 cm (2 feet) deep. When planting, leave enough room in the top of the container so that an extra 10 cm (4 inches) of soil can be added when the new stems are 15 cm (6 inches) tall.

# Rhubarb

Perhaps one of the easiest crops to grow, rhubarb is robust, mostly free of pests and diseases, and will withstand some neglect. It can also cope with a degree of shade, and once established you can leave it where it is for a good number of years without needing to replant.

**LIFESPAN**
Perennial

**PLANT**
Plant transplants or divisions as soon as soil can be worked in early spring

**GROW IN**
Prefers a rich, moisture-retentive soil, but most soil is fine. Copes well with shade

## Planting Tips

It is possible to grow rhubarb from seeds, but these are usually not the best eating cultivars. Because the plants last for a long time, and the crowns can be divided to multiply stock, I recommend spending money on getting good strong plants of a really good cultivar.

## Cultivation

Keep well watered in the first year. Once established, plants have deep roots and tolerate periods of drought. They are heavy feeders, however, so mulch with aged compost every year.

## Weed Control

It is vital that all perennial weeds are removed before planting, but otherwise rhubarb is one of the best weed-smothering crops. You will only need to weed by hand occasionally. I even lay the leaves of the harvested stems around other plants as a mulch to help control weeds.

## Harvest

There is a lot of conflicting advice when it comes to harvesting rhubarb. The truth is that you can pick pretty much any time after the first year, when it's best to leave the plant alone so that it can become established and build up some reserves. The stalks can get tough when it gets dry, so I usually stop picking in early summer.

## Container Tip

Rhubarb is not recommended for growing in a container because it likes to get its roots deep into the ground.

# Squash

I love growing and eating squash, but their success does depend on climate and variety. There is a massive range, from the quick-maturing summer onion squashes to the hardy winter varieties. Stored carefully, you could be eating them for most of the winter.

**LIFESPAN**
Annual

**PLANT**
Sow indoors in seed flats two weeks before the last expected frost, or directly outdoors in early summer

**GROW IN**
Rich, well-drained soil in full sun

## Planting Tips

In my experience, squash mostly performs better if sown directly in the ground, provided you have a warm enough climate; the seeds need a minimum of 13°C (56°F ) to germinate. Starting in protected conditions inside can give you a head start, but the plants usually get "checked" when you plant them outdoors and take a week or two before they start growing again.

## Cultivation

Squash like the weather hot and dry, but with frequent watering at the roots. The plants will suffer if the nights get cold, particularly in the early stages of development. Feeding with a balanced liquid fertilizer will increase yields, and it is essential for container crops.

## Weed Control

Plant squash seedlings through cardboard around the plants. Alternatively, keep the surrounding soil free of weeds in the initial stages. Once they get going, they smother most weeds. The plants can also be undersown with a low-growing leguminous cover crop.

## Harvest

Summer squash should be harvested as they are ready, but for winter squash it is important that the skins harden before harvesting. This normally means waiting until the leaves have died back, preferably before there is a hard frost. In some climates, this is a short window of opportunity. Push a fingernail gently into the skin of the squash; if it doesn't leave a mark, then it's ready to be harvested.

## Container Tip

Squash grow well in containers, provided you add plenty of rich soil mix (they will actually grow well in pure aged compost), and water and feed regularly.

# Sweetcorn

Although it takes up a lot of space in a plot, there is nothing quite like freshly harvested sweetcorn—it is so much sweeter than cobs that have been hanging around on trucks and store shelves for days.

**LIFESPAN**
Annual

**PLANT**
Sow directly in spring after danger of frost is past or in pots or trays in mid- to late spring a week before planting outdoors

**GROW IN**
Rich, well-drained soil in a hot, sunny, sheltered site

## Planting Tips

If growing in seed flats instead of larger individual pots, be sure you plant outside quickly because seedlings have powerful root systems that quickly outgrow flats. I prefer sowing directly into the soil and find they usually catch up with earlier, pot-sown plants. Sweetcorn is pollinated by the wind, so it tends to be more successful planted in a block instead of in a long single row.

## Cultivation

Sweetcorn is a hungry plant, so feed the soil well before planting. While it thrives in hot, dry weather and can cope with dry conditions, it pays to keep the soil moist once the crop starts to flower—particularly in drought years.

## Weed Control

The plants grow tall quickly, so weeds are rarely a problem. Sometimes they are sown at a slightly wider spacing—for example, 60 cm (24 inches) apart instead of 45 cm (18 inches) apart—so that weed-smothering plants, such as trailing squash, can be interplanted between the sweetcorn.

## Harvest

When the tassels (which are the stamens of the corn flowers) become dry and turn brown, it is the main sign that the cob is ready to pick. Check that the whole cob has filled out: give the top end a gentle squeeze, and it should feel rounded. If it feels pointy, then it's not ready.

## Container Tip

You can grow sweetcorn in containers, but you will need deep ones, and you might struggle with pollination unless you have a lot of containers full of sweetcorn bunched together.

# Tomatoes

**LIFESPAN**
Annual

**PLANT**
Sow directly in spring after danger of frost is past or in pots or trays in mid- to late spring a week before planting outdoors

**GROW IN**
Rich, well-drained soil in a hot, sunny, sheltered site

There's really no reason not to grow tomatoes. With the right choice of variety, they will taste vastly superior to those you buy in stores. They are relatively easy to grow, although feeding and watering is important.

## Planting Tips

I sow the seeds in flats or pots and then transplant the stronger seedlings into individual pots to continue growing. Sometimes I transplant them into a larger pot before planting into their final space. They will root from the stem, so plant them a little deeper to allow for a larger root area.

## Cultivation

Tomatoes need rich soil, but if your soil is not there yet, you can supplement with a natural liquid fertilizer high in potassium and phosphorus. Water with a solution of this once the flowers start to form. Avoid high-nitrogen fertilizers because they will make the growth sappy, lush, and susceptible to disease and pest attack. Regular but not excessive watering is essential if you want to avoid split fruit. Stop watering in autumn to help prevent fungal diseases as the weather gets cooler and damper. Remove the lower leaves as they start to discolor; this allows for the plant to put all its energy into the younger, productive growth and the developing fruit. Support the growth as the plants begin to grow upward, and remove the side shoots of vine tomatoes so that only the main stem grows up the support.

## Weed Control

Keep weeds at bay, especially at the early stages. Young plants can be planted through cardboard, or you can cover the soil with a layer of organic mulch. Try undersowing with marigolds (*Calendula officinalis*); as well as smothering weeds, they are also said to attract beneficial insects that can deter some pests.

## Harvest

Harvest regularly. If you are eating the fruit immediately, then leave it on the plant until completely ripe. Pick a couple of days early if you need to transport or keep the fruit. At the end of the season, pick any green tomatoes and bring them indoors for ripening in a warm place.

## Container Tip

Tomatoes grow well in containers, although attention to feeding and watering is important.

# Flowers for Eating and Cutting

Beautiful in both the garden and the house, and fantastic for wildlife, flowers can also add real colour and character to salads, oils, and more. Some, such as nasturtiums, have a punchy peppery flavour, while others, such as violets, are more subtle.

## Harvest

**FOR EATING** Try to harvest on a dry morning. The flowers should be plump but not wet. Too dry, and they wilt before you get them home; too wet, and they will rot quickly. Petals are generally delicate and need to be handled with extreme care. I pick them and put them into a small basket, which I don't fill to more than two blooms deep.

Don't leave cut flowers in the sun, even for a few minutes, because they will quickly wilt. Get them chilled as quickly as possible.

**FOR THE VASE** Although whole stems are cut (instead of just individual flowers), it is still best to do so in the morning, when the stems are at their most fresh. Cut stems long—for most plants, this means at the bottom of the stem—and get them into a pail of water as soon as possible. Try to cut before the flower is completely opened so that they last as long as possible.

## Safety

Unlike most of our fruit and vegetables, which are bred specifically for human consumption, flowers are developed mainly for ornamental benefit. I have listed some on pages 144–149 as fine to eat (as are many more), but there are some other flowers that are either poisonous or just not that nice. If in doubt, either don't eat them or do more research first. Some flowers used for cutting can cause a rash, so it is advisable to wear gloves when picking them.

## Fruit/Vegetable Flowers

Even if you don't want to devote precious space in your community garden to cut flowers, there are some you might be already growing that can double up as cut flowers or foliage. Most of the alliums, such as leeks and onions, for example, produce wonderful-looking spherical flowers, and the flower heads of carrots, celery, and other members of the carrot family are delicate and pretty. Rocket flowers are lovely, although they don't last long, but generally it is best to avoid most other brassica flowers, because they can smell of cabbage once in a vase. Asparagus foliage works well as a feathery foil to cut flowers.

# Annuals and Biennials

It is easy to propagate and plant annual flowers among vegetable crops. They are usually sown in spring or early summer and grow quickly before flowering. Biennials will spend the first year growing and will flower in the second. Many of them are usually regarded as border flowers.

**PLANT**
Most types are sown in spring, although some biennials do well from a late-summer sowing

**GROW IN**
Most soil types, including poorer soil, usually in full sun

## Planting Tips

Annuals and biennials tend to germinate easily and grow quickly. They can be sown directly into the ground or into seed flats and transplanted. The latter works well in cooler climates for less frost-hardy cultivars.

## Cultivation

Most of these plants are basically straightforward, although if you can give them water in dry conditions, you will probably get higher yields over a longer period. In many cases, with sweet peas for example, the regular removal of flowers for cutting can encourage additional flowering. Biennials need particular attention to make sure they are not "lost," neglected, or simply forgotten about over the winter months; at the beginning of their second season, they can be moved to a new location if this is what is required.

## Weed Control

As with vegetables, some of these flowers compete well with weeds and others don't. It is best to always give them a good, weed-free start and then weed by hand or hoe, when necessary, until they are established. With biennials, the bed will need to be kept free of weeds all through the first year to give the plants the best chance of survival into their second year.

## Suggested Varieties

**FOR EATING:** *Calendula*, *Tagetes*, *Viola*, *Petunia*, and *Antirrhinum* all have edible flowers.

Don't forget that many vegetables can also be harvested at the floral stage. Green beans, cucumbers, squash, radishes, rocket, and many more all have delicious flowers. You can often harvest the flower without affecting the yield of the main vegetable, effectively giving you a double crop.

**FOR THE VASE:** Poppies and *Nigella* will give only one cutting, while others, such as *Ammi*, *Cosmos*, sweet peas, and multiheaded sunflowers, can produce flowers over a long period—if you continue to keep cutting and stimulating new growth.

Biennials sweet William (*Dianthus barbatus*) and *Erysimum* sown in midsummer and grown through the winter give a lovely display starting early the next spring, and they are usually highly scented. Picked regularly, they will keep flowering until it gets hot in summer.

## Container Tips

Almost all annuals and biennials do well in containers and will often cope with short periods without water. When they are spent, the container is easily replanted or moved away.

# Perennials and Bulbs

Many perennials and bulbs work well as both edible and cut flowers. A perennial is any plant that lives for more than two years, where the plants usually die back to ground level during winter. When they are dormant, bulbs survive underground until conditions become favourable.

**PLANT**
Purchase young plants or bulbs and plant them when dormant during late autumn or early spring

**GROW IN**
Perennials mostly benefit from a rich soil. Bulbs typically prefer well-drained soil. Situate in full sun

## Planting Tips

If bought in pots, bulbs and perennials can be planted at any time of the year. The clumping types will need occasional dividing. Dig up the root ball when the plant is dormant and divide into smaller sections for replanting. Extra divisions can be given away or sold to raise funds for your community garden.

## Cultivation

Plants tend to flower more readily when they are under stress. So, although some require rich soil, if you are growing for flowers, you can often use poorer soil or some that is at the end of the rotation.

## Weed Control

Perennials are usually best kept free of weeds, mainly because it makes their management much simpler. Bulbs are best enjoyed and harvested on ground that is clear of weeds. Mulch well with aged compost or wood chips and occasionally weed by hand.

## Suggested Varieties

**FOR EATING** Dandelions, daylilies, tulips and chives all have edible flowers. As the name suggests, individual daylily flowers last just one day, so it makes sense to make use of them in the kitchen. Thanks to modern breeding, tulips can be chosen in almost any colour.

**FOR THE VASE** There are a great number of perennials that would be suitable for cutting. Some last longer than others in a vase, but try what you like. *Delphinium* is a particular favourite of mine. *Echinops*, *Phlox*, and *Helenium* are beautiful and easy, too. Almost all ferns work well for their distinctive foliage. Lilies, irises, astrantias, and chrysanthemums are also good choices, and the list goes on and on.

## Container Tips

Bulbs generally do well in containers, as do the smaller perennials. Larger ones, such as *Delphinium*, need a deeper, rich soil and don't do as well, but they can be grown in large containers with plenty of water and staking.

# Trees and Shrubs

Sometimes forgotten in the cut-flower
department, trees and shrubs not only
provide lovely leaves and beautiful blooms
and berries, but even stunning stems. They
provide permanent structure in a community
garden and will encourage wildlife.

**LIFESPAN**
Long-lived perennials

**PLANT**
During late autumn or early
spring. Provided the weather
is relatively mild, container
plants can be planted
any time of year

**GROW IN**
Most like a rich, well-drained
soil; some will be better suited
to difficult conditions

## Planting Tips

Because they will probably be in the
ground for a long time, first make sure
the tree or shrub you choose is suited
to the site. It is vital that you prepare
the ground well and provide plenty of
water on planting to help the soil settle
around the roots.

## Cultivation

New trees and shrubs most certainly
need watering during the first year,
whether or not the weather is dry. In
most climates, the plants should be
able to look after themselves by year
two. Each year, check the canopy for
dead, diseased, or wayward branches
and prune them out. Flowering shrubs
or trees must be clipped or pruned
only after flowering, or else you risk
removing the coming flower buds.

## Weed Control

If possible, keep the ground weeded
around the bottom of the trunk for
the first couple of years. It is a good
idea to spread a thick mulch of well-
aged compost around the trunk after
planting to lock in moisture, but keep
the trunk itself clear of mulch. Smaller
cultivars need weeding for their entire
lives. A yearly application of wood-
chip mulch works well.

## Suggested Choices

**FOR EATING:** Apple, plum, and
elderflower are just a few of the trees
with edible flowers that you might
already have in your garden. It's also no
surprise that the shrubby herbs sage,
thyme, and rosemary all have edible
flowers. One chef I used to supply paid
me more for fresh young thyme flowers

than for the herb itself because he loved their peppery tang.

**FOR THE VASE:** Coloured dogwoods (*Cornus*) and willows are invaluable for their winter stems. Forsythias, lilacs, witch hazel, viburnums, and *Callicarpa* have great flowers. Trees and shrubs are also great for foliage; try coppiced eucalyptus, as well as *Acer*, *Euonymus*, *Elaeagnus*, or *Pittosporum*, and don't forget holly and other evergreens for the Christmas season. The delicate silvery leaves of *Artemisia* are a favourite among florists.

## Container Tips

Smaller trees and shrubs can work well in large containers, but almost all tend to do better in the soil if you have the space to plant them in the ground.

# Currants and Gooseberries

Currants and gooseberries are probably one of the easiest to grow of the soft fruits, and you'll find they all require similar treatment. They can host white pine blister rust which is an issue in some countries, so always check before planting.

**LIFESPAN**
Short-lived perennials

**PLANT**
Transport while dormant (with no leaves) and plant in autumn or very early spring

**GROW IN**
Any well-drained, fertile soil, preferably in sun, but they tolerate some shade

## Types

**BLACK CURRANTS** The stems of these bushes grow from the base and produce fruit mostly on one- or two-year-old wood. They are the most vigorous of the currants and can grow large if left unpruned. The currants have a rich flavour and a high vitamin C content, and they make a superb jelly. Birds don't seem as fond of black currants as they are of the softer white currants and red currants.

**JOSTABERRIES** A cross between black currants and gooseberries, jostaberries grow and look like black currants but have a larger fruit with a slightly milder flavour.

**RED CURRANTS AND WHITE CURRANTS** The bright and highly colourful currants make these shrubs ornamental when they are in season, but they are equally eye-catching to birds, so provide protection. With a softer berry than the black currant, they don't last as long, and you will need to harvest more gently.

**GOOSEBERRIES** The bigger berry on gooseberries makes harvesting easier, although it is also slightly more dangerous due to the long prickles that cover the branches. Gooseberries are a little more prone to pests and diseases, such as sawfly caterpillars and mildew.

If I were to grow only one of these, I would choose the black currant for ease of use and flavour.

## Planting Tips

Prepare the ground well, removing all weeds, and water in well on planting. Spread a mulch of good aged compost around the plant once it is in the ground. With the exception of black currants, currants and gooseberries should be planted at the same depth that they were in their original pot. Plant black currants slightly deeper because it encourages new shoots to grow from the base.

To increase your stock of plants, you can take hardwood cuttings from healthy plants in late winter. Cut off a few 20–25-cm (8–10-inch) sections of healthy stem and stick them in the ground the right way up. As they grow, keep them watered, and, with some luck, a few of them will take. It's a cheap way of getting more plants.

## Cultivation

Water plants in dry periods, particularly when the fruit are developing, and spread a mulch of aged compost around the roots every year to keep the soil fertile. In winter, prune carefully to create an open vase shape, removing congested growth and shortening wayward stems. On black currants, remove about one-third of the older shoots at ground level to encourage productive new growth. When it comes to training, white currants, red currants, and gooseberries are adaptable. They can be trained in a number of ways, which is useful where space is restricted. For example, they can be trained as a fan along wires against a wall or fence. Growing them like this can also help reduce fungal diseases due to better airflow around the leaves. Black currants, however, cannot be trained and must be grown as a bush. Currants and gooseberries will do well in shady spots.

## Weed Control

You can grow shallow ground-cover plants, such as strawberries or herbs, around the base of these plants. These will smother weeds without competing with the bushes. Alternatively, lay cardboard around the root zone and cover with a thick mulch layer to exclude weeds and conserve moisture.

## Harvest

The trick with currants and gooseberries is to get them before the birds do. You may need to net the whole crop during the fruit-producing season or grow them in a fruit cage. They mostly ripen within the space of a few weeks so you should be able to clear the bushes in two or three picks. I lay out the berries one layer thick on a tray, freeze them, and then repack them in containers. You can then help yourself from the freezer to as many or as few as you like, when you like. You can add the frozen currants to cake mixes, gelatins, and sauces later in the year.

## Container Tip

Most currants and gooseberries grow well in large containers, although black currants and jostaberries may struggle if they are not fed and watered regularly.

# Raspberries

Perhaps my favourite soft fruit to eat, the raspberry is easy enough to grow but delicate and hard to keep in good condition once picked. This makes it expensive to buy in grocery stores but perfect for community gardens, where it can be eaten on site.

**LIFESPAN**
Perennial

**PLANT**
As bare-root "canes," while dormant in winter

**GROW IN**
Any well-drained, fertile soil in sun or part shade

## Planting Tips

Plant so that the top roots are about 5 cm (2 inches) below ground level but be careful not to plant too deep; space each plant 35–45 cm (14–18 inches) apart. Cut the canes back to about 15 cm (6 inches) if they haven't already been pruned.

## Cultivation

The raspberry is naturally a woodland edge plant that, in the wild, would "creep" as margins of the woods expanded. This leads to suckers forming and a dislike of growing in straight rows. If you have an area where you can let it run wild, it will thrive, although it may make harvesting and weeding a little more difficult. It may be sensible to control the number of new canes to keep the crop manageable and to produce less, but higher-quality, fruit.

## Weed Control

Weeding raspberries is notoriously difficult. It is best to control weeds using thick organic mulches. Try to make sure that there are no perennial weeds in the ground before planting, and keep on top of weeds by hand-weeding and mulching.

## Harvest

Raspberries are best when harvested straight into the mouth after washing. If you do have to package them, place them straight into a small container at a maximum of two fruit deep (a single layer is better). The less you handle the fruit, the better. Place the fruit in a cool place within a half hour of picking to keep fresh for longer.

## Container Tip

Although tall plants, raspberries have shallow roots, so provided you have a relatively large container, you can grow them successfully. Keep them well watered and fed.

# Blueberries

Blueberries are a great plant for containers; in many areas, this is the only way to grow them because they are particular about needing acidic soil. They are great for community gardens with children, who love to help with picking—and eating—the berries.

**LIFESPAN**
Perennial

**PLANT**
Two- or three-year-old plants are planted in late autumn or early spring

**GROW IN**
Acidic, well-drained soil of pH 5.5 or less is essential; in containers, use an ericaceous soil mix. Choose a sunny site

## Planting Tips

If you are growing in the ground, do a soil test to be sure the pH (acidity level) is 5.5 or less. Simple test kits are available from plant retailers, but if you want to be sure, you can send samples of your soil to a soil testing laboratory to get a full picture of what is in your soil.

## Cultivation

If the soil pH is right, then blueberries grow easily with few pests and diseases. After a couple of years, you will need to do some pruning to make sure there is enough productive growth. Prune in early spring, removing two or three of the older branches to ground level to encourage new growth. Keep the plants well watered, using collected rainwater (which contains much less lime than tap water), particularly if you are growing in containers, and then spread a mulch of pine needles or bark chip around the root zone. If the leaves begin to yellow, water with a specialist ericaceous liquid feed. Repot blueberries in containers every two to three years, and always refresh the soil each time.

## Weed Control

Blueberries are generally easy to weed, by hand or careful hoeing, but always work carefully because they have shallow roots.

## Harvest

The berries are easy to pick by hand. If you have a lot of plants, consider buying a berry picker tool, which is a kind of forked scoop that you can run over the bushes to collect the fruit. The harvest will be improved if you can grow two or more plants together, because the shrubs will be able to pollinate each other.

## Container Tips

Blueberries are ideal for pots, because they are small shrubs that cope well with some root restriction. Keep well watered—and enjoy the autumn colour.

# Strawberries

Quick to fruit and easy to grow, I would include strawberries in almost any community gardening plan, even if it's just a few plants to give your members a summer treat. Nothing beats the "fresh from the bush" experience, especially if you choose some really tasty cultivars.

**LIFESPAN**
Short-lived perennial

**PLANT**
Grow from plants in spring;
in mild-winter areas,
plant in early autumn

**GROW IN**
A rich, moist soil in full sun

## Planting Tips

Plant in spring to give the plants time to get established by winter, but if you live in a mild-winter area, an early autumn planting will bring fruit the next summer. You can also separate runners from existing plants five to six weeks after they appear to establish new plants, but limit this to five from the mother plant and one from the new runner plant, as the quality of the fruit will gradually decline.

Grow a range of cultivars to have a long harvest season, but pick ones that you are unlikely to find in the stores. Choose from "everbearing" cultivars that provide a longer picking season, although the fruit will be smaller. You can also plant a couple of "June bearers" for a heavy crop of large fruit over a short period. Everbearing types are less popular commercially because you have to go over the same bushes more often for the same crop, but they work well for community gardens where little and often can be an advantage.

## Cultivation

Keep the plants well watered, but avoid overhead watering as the fruit develop because this may cause them to rot. Using a balanced liquid fertilizer at this time will improve the quality and quantity of the fruit. Remove runners as they appear, unless you are propagating them for more plants. Strawberries are prone to slug damage, and when they turn red, they are readily picked at by birds, so protect the crop with netting.

You can keep growing strawberry plants for a few years, but as they get older, the fruit tends to get smaller. This means more picking for the same quantity of fruit. For this reason, as well as avoiding disease buildup, replanting is generally recommended every three years or so.

## Weed Control

Strawberries don't compete that well with weeds, so they are usually grown through a mulch of either straw or

woody mulch. This helps to retain moisture and protect the fruit. In late winter or early spring, tidy the plants by removing the old foliage and taking out any weeds by hand.

## Harvest

When the time comes, pick the fruit often, and always remove rotten or half-eaten fruit because these will cause disease problems for the remaining crop.

## Container Tip

Strawberries are wonderful container plants. Being small and hardy, you can even grow them in small containers, provided that they have enough food and water.

# Melons

Being related to courgette and other squash, sweet melons are cultivated in almost the same way. Traditionally grown in warmer climates or under cover, there are new cultivars that make them a possibility even for some cool conditions.

**LIFESPAN**
Annual

**PLANT**
Wait until after the last frost if growing outside in a cool climate; otherwise, in spring after danger of frost has past

**GROW IN**
A rich, well-drained soil in full sun

## Planting Tips

Melons hate cold ground, so make sure that your soil is at least 21°C (70°F) before planting. In cold climates, repotting into a larger pot in a greenhouse before planting outside is advisable.

## Cultivation

It is possible to train melons up trellis or wire, although you need to be careful not to damage the stems. This not only helps to reduce disease by increasing airflow, but it also allows more sun to reach the fruit, which will help them ripen. Melons need regular watering, especially just after being planted and when the fruit first start forming.

## Weed Control

As with squash, keep melons weeded while they establish. Once the vines start growing, you shouldn't have any problems with weeds, although growing through a cardboard and mulch cuts out all weeding and helps to keep much-needed moisture in.

## Harvest

Melons are really sweet, so a lot of animals like to eat them. Keep the fruit off the ground to avoid the smaller pests; you may need to protect them with a crate if you have problems with larger animals stealing them.

## Container Tips

Melons grow well in containers, provided they are warm and moist enough. Start them indoors or in a greenhouse and then move the pot outside to provide a longer season.

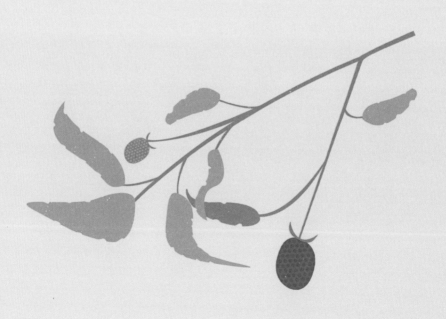

# Blackberries and Hybrid Berries

This group includes tayberries and loganberries. They take up a fair amount of space in the garden, although they can be kept within bounds by training against walls or wires.

**LIFESPAN**
Perennials

**PLANT**
As bare-root "canes," late autumn in mild-winter areas or early spring in cold-winter areas

**GROW IN**
Any well-drained, fertile soil in sun or part shade

## Planting Tips

The canes appreciate being planted in a soil that has been well dug over, with all weeds removed. Put supports or wires in place before planting and then dig a good hole for each, watering in well as you backfill and then mulch with plenty of rotted compost. Vigorous cultivars will need wider spacing than less-vigorous types; a distance of 2.5–3.5 m (8–11½ feet) between plants is a guide.

## Cultivation

Fruit appears on last year's growth, so cut back the old, fruited wood every year and then train in the new shoots as they grow, ready to produce in the following season. The new shoots grow quickly and may reach 3 cm (10 feet) long, so give them plenty of room or cut them to fit the space you have. The main problem for traditional blackberries are their thorns, but luckily there is a growing range of thornless cultivars available with bigger, juicier berries.

## Weed Control

These vigorous plants outgrow most weeds, but pull out any large weeds as they appear. It is possible to make use of the space beneath the canes to grow a low-growing ground cover or cover crop.

## Harvest

Make sure the maturing crop is protected with netting; birds go for hybrid berries, although blackberries seem less prone. Pick as soon as the berries are ripe, because they quickly rot if left. As with raspberries, eat, chill, or freeze them immediately.

## Container Tip

With their vigorous root system, these berries need a big container to do well. Some of the thornless cultivars are slightly less vigorous.

# Ground Cherries

Plants of *Physalis* spp. provide golden cherry-sized fruits. Easy to grow, these relatives of the tomato and tomatillo look great as a garnish and come in their own protective layer—perfect for selling or packing in boxes.

**LIFESPAN**
Short-lived perennial in frost-free areas

**PLANT**
Sow the seeds indoors in high humidity in spring at 18°C (65°F)

**GROW IN**
Copes or even thrives in poor, well-drained soils, in a frost-free and sunny position

## Planting Tips

Plant seedlings in their final locations only after all risk of frost is past. If the soil is too fertile, the plant will probably produce a lot of foliage but little in the way of fruit.

## Cultivation

Perfect for beginners or less than perfect sites, ground cherries will cope with a little neglect. Good harvests are possible even in the most unlikely spots, although it does need a fair amount of water. The plants can reach up to 1.8 m (6 feet) tall and might need some support. A strong main stake, or a few stakes with string tied across them, will help to prevent the branches from breaking.

## Weed Control

Ground cherries are vigorous plants that will outcompete most weeds. While they are young, a quick weeding around the plants by hand or hoe should be enough.

## Harvest

The season varies widely depending on climate, and can be anytime from early summer to early autumn. Harvest the fruit once it drops, but be aware that it may not be completely ripe at this stage. Knowing exactly which ones are ripe comes with experience. Just peel back the papery cover to check the colour of the fruit.

## Container Tip

The plants grow well in containers, and because they don't need particularly fertile soil, I sometimes plant one in an old container using soil from one of last season's crops. In areas that experience frost over winter, move the pot to a sheltered position during the cold season.

# Apples

Apples are probably the most common fruit tree to be planted in temperate areas, partly because they are easy to grow and produce well, and there is a huge number of delicious cultivars to choose from. Dwarf trees can be grown in containers or small spaces.

LIFESPAN
Perennial

PLANT
Bare-root plants are planted in late autumn or early spring

GROW IN
Any fertile, well-drained soil

## Planting Tips

To get the soil right before planting, dig the ground over and remove weeds, and then prepare a planting hole a bit deeper than the tree roots so that the graft union (where the rootstock meets the top growth, usually visible as a small bulge) is just above ground level. Water in well as you backfill and firm around the roots with your heel. Finally, add a mulch of aged compost around the tree.

## Cultivation

Keep well watered in the first year after planting, even if the weather is cool. Once established, trees on all but the smallest dwarf stock (or those in containers) should cope without watering. Pruning will help ensure a healthy and productive tree. Remove crossing or wayward branches and shorten new shoots by half or one-third to encourage production.

## Weed Control

It is vital to maintain a weed-free area in the root zone, at least for the first couple of years. Once established, the trees will be able to cope with some ground cover around the trunk.

## Harvest

Exact harvest times for each cultivar will vary from region to region and year to year. Either check regularly to see if the fruit comes off easily in your hand, or wait for the first fruit to drop and then harvest them all. Keep records to make planning for harvest easier in future years.

## Container Tips

Use a dwarf tree for container growing, or else the tree will quickly become rootbound. Feed annually when the leaves begin to grow, and keep the soil just moist.

# Pears

Pears have broadly the same planting and growing requirements as apples, but there are a few important differences. Pears cope well in heavier soil but are more frost- and drought-sensitive than apples. Also, they are usually slower to produce but will live for longer than apples.

**LIFESPAN**
Perennial

**PLANT**
Bare-root plants are planted in late autumn or early spring

**GROW IN**
Most fertile, well-drained soil, but avoid those that are chalky or sandy

## Planting Tips

Plant as for apples, but keep in mind that pears, even more than apples, like wind protection—so if you have an exposed site, it's worth planting or constructing an effective windbreak well before the pears go in. Even in areas with a lot of neighbouring yards, consider planting at least two compatible trees for pollination, because it will help greatly with fruit set. Most garden centres will advise you on which to choose.

## Cultivation

As for any new tree, keep the ground well watered in the first year after planting, even if the weather is cool. This will help the roots get established, after which the trees should be able to fend for themselves unless they are container-grown. As with apple trees, pears benefit from an annual prune to maintain a healthy, uncongested branching structure.

## Weed Control

Keep the root zone free of weeds, at least for the first couple of years. Once established, the trees will be able to cope with some ground cover around the trunk.

## Harvest

Hold the fruit in your palm and give it an upward twist; if the stem comes away from the tree easily, it's ready to pick, although it may still need some time to ripen. For later cultivars in autumn, pick when hard (cut the stems if they do not pull off easily) and store until they ripen. Unlike apples, it's harder to keep pears for more than a couple of months in store. Bring a few fruit in at a time into a warmer room to continue the final ripening.

## Container Tips

Pears on dwarf rootstocks grow well in containers. However, they do not like drying out, so keep them well watered, particularly during blossom and fruit formation. Feed annually when the leaves begin to grow in spring.

# Plums

Plum trees blossom and set fruit relatively early, and because a late frost can devastate an entire crop at the developmental stage, the trees are best planted in a warm and protected site. Otherwise, plums are easy to grow and perfect for community gardens.

**LIFESPAN**
Perennial

**PLANT**
Plant in late autumn or early spring

**GROW IN**
Any fertile soil that is well drained—they hate wet feet

## Planting Tips

Choose plum trees suitable to the climate in which you live. European plums have the tastiest fruit but need a temperate climate that isn't too hot or cold. Frost-sensitive Japanese plums will thrive in the same climates as peaches. American hybrids—a cross between Japanese plums and tart American plums—are best for cold-winter gardens. Although many plums are self fertile, check before buying that the one you are choosing is not one that needs a partner tree for pollination. If it is, plant two trees at a spacing of 3–5 m (10–15 feet) apart.

## Cultivation

Water trees well during their first year to help them establish. Thereafter, water only during periods of drought and as the fruit is swelling, and begin to prune the trees to shape as they develop. A great way to grow plums is to train them as a fan on a south or southwest facing wall, which gives extra warmth and protection. They are also more easily covered by a floating row cover for early frost protection and by netting during harvest to keep the birds away. Due to their sensitivity to bacterial infections, it's recommended to prune only in summer, when the damage heals more quickly.

## Weed Control

Keep the area around the root zone well weeded in the first couple of years. It will make a huge difference to the development of the tree.

## Harvest

Treat plums like berries—they need to be harvested and eaten immediately. It is possible to pick a little early, letting the last few days' ripening take place indoors, but they are never as good.

## Container Tip

There are dwarf rootstocks that make container growing possible, but it's more difficult than apples or pears. If possible, grow plums in the soil.

# Cherries

Unless you plan to grow a cooking (or acidic) cultivar of cherries, which is less palatable fresh, you must make provision for a net to cover your crop at harvest time. There is now a range of relatively compact, self-fertile cultivars that take less effort to contain.

**LIFESPAN**
Perennial

**PLANT**
Plant in early spring

**GROW IN**
A deep, well-drained, and fertile soil

## Planting Tips

Consider planting at least a couple of trees, because even self-fertile cultivars tend to yield more if another tree is nearby. Acidic cultivars don't mind some shade and can even be grown well on a shady wall, but sweet cherries must have full sun to get the sugar content up. Dwarf trees will need staking, often for their entire life, because their dwarf rootstocks do not have strong root systems. They are also more susceptible to wind damage and drought.

## Cultivation

Water trees well during their first year to help them establish. Thereafter, water routinely during dry periods in spring and summer to be sure that there is a reliable source of moisture for the developing fruit. A soaker hose partly buried under the soil close to the trees makes this task simpler. You can train cherries into a fan shape against a large wall or onto a wire framework, which it makes it easier to net the trees and protect them from frost. As with plums, prune the trees in summer to reduce the chance of bacterial infection.

## Weed Control

Keep the area around the root zone well weeded in the first couple of years. It will make a huge difference to the development of the tree.

## Harvest

There is only a small picking window for cherries, so check daily when the fruit starts to turn red. As with most fruit, if you can pick in dry weather conditions, the fruit will last longer. Try to avoid touching the fruit itself, which will damage easily, but hold the stem and place straight into shallow trays. Sweet cultivars will keep for perhaps a week if you chill them immediately after harvest, while sour cherries are best cooked or frozen immediately.

## Container Tips

If you have shallow or sandy soil, it is better to grow a cherry tree in a big container. Smaller cultivars and rootstocks are ideal for container planting, although they need regular watering, especially at blossom and fruiting. You will also need to pile on a layer of good-quality aged compost at least once a year to keep them fed.

# Grapes

The plants themselves are frost-hardy (they need at least one month in winter below 4°C /40°F), but the fruit need a lot of warmth and sun to ripen well. In cool climates, it is sometimes best to grow them under glass for a good crop. It is worth it for the intense flavour of sun-ripened grapes.

**LIFESPAN**
Perennial

**PLANT**
Bare-root plants are planted in early spring, container-grown ones in spring or autumn

**GROW IN**
Any free-draining soil in full sun

## Planting Tips

Grape vines are climbing plants, so they need to be trained onto some kind of support. They do not need a rich soil, but it must be free draining; once the roots get into the subsoil, they are able to scavenge well for nutrients, and, indeed, it is with a degree of benign neglect that you can grow the best-flavoured grapes. For higher yield, however, some growers will irrigate and feed their crops.

## Cultivation

Water well upon planting and for the first year. Thereafter, provide a thick mulch of compost around the roots, but do not allow the mulch to build up around the main stem. To improve airflow and get the right amount of fruit, the vines need pruning each year. It must be done in winter, when the plant is dormant—if left too late, the cut shoots will weep considerably, draining the plant of energy. Typically, a vine is pruned back to a bare framework of just a few main stems—or even one—but there are a number of different styles. From the main stem(s), side shoots will grow each year; clip these back to about five leaves in early summer so that just one bunch of fruit is allowed to develop on each side shoot.

## Weed Control

Grape vines are climbers, so they are largely unaffected by weeds, but any extra growth around the main stems can reduce airflow and lead to an increased risk of disease in wetter climates. For this reason, the area around the stems is usually kept clear.

## Harvest

A good guide is to taste one of the grapes to determine if they are ready to pick. Then, use pruners to cut the whole stem at once.

## Container Tip

The vines can grow well in pots and can be trained as standards but they do have vigorous roots. A big container and regular watering are vital.

# Figs

Worth trying if you have plenty of space, figs are vigorous trees that are hardy down to -10°C (14°F). Getting them to produce reliably can be a problem. There is sometimes a lot of leaf and not many figs, and at other times a lot of fruit that does not ripen if the summer is not long enough.

**LIFESPAN**
Perennial

**PLANT**
Spring is the best time

**GROW IN**
Most types of well-drained soil

## Planting Tips

Figs are normally sold in containers, so dig a good planting hole and tease the roots out from the root ball and, if necessary, break or cut ones that have started growing around the inside of the pot. Fill the hole back in with soil and water in well as you work. During the first year, keep the roots well watered, even during the cool weather.

In deep, rich soil, the planting hole is sometimes lined with concrete slabs to restrict root growth and control the size of the tree. However, if you want to have a big tree, or you have poor soil, this isn't essential.

## Cultivation

Figs can manage without a lot of water. However, if you want to improve the potential harvest, water occasionally throughout summer, particularly if the plant is growing in a restricted hole or in a container. Irregular or erratic watering, however, can make the fruit split, so be careful to water regularly but not excessively.

## Weed Control

Initially, keep young or newly planted trees weeded. You will find that their vigorous growth will soon outcompete most weeds.

## Harvest

It's not hard to see if a fig is ready. Some will turn brown and feel soft when squeezed, and a sticky drop may even ooze from their base. Be careful that birds do not snatch or peck at the fruit before you have a chance to get to it yourself—net the crop, if necessary.

## Container Tip

Growing in a container is a good way to restrict the root system and overall size of a fig tree, and it will also encourage fruit production. The downside is that it will need careful watering, particularly when the fruit forms and swells.

# Coriander

With its intense flavour, coriander (sometimes called "cilantro") is one of those herbs that can totally transform a dish, particularly those needing a Middle Eastern or North African flavour. It germinates and grows easily, and you can also eat the seeds, what's not to love?

**LIFESPAN**
Annual

**PLANT**
Sow where they are to grow in spring and autumn; in mild-summer areas, in summer, too

**GROW IN**
Most soil is suitable

## Planting Tips

Coriander will germinate at temperatures as low as 13°C (55°F), so it can be sown outdoors from spring in most climates and under a floating row cover even earlier. It has a large seed and, therefore, is easy to sow and handle. Aim to sow regularly for a succession of fresh leaves through the summer. Those crops that go to flower can be left for their seeds or pulled out to make room for something else.

## Cultivation

The only downside with coriander is that it has a tendency to go to seed (bolt) in all but the coolest, dampest conditions. Extremes in temperature have a similar effect. Irrigation is, therefore, crucial, because without it, the crop will bolt. For this reason, you may find you have more success with an earlier crop.

## Weed control

Coriander germinates quickly and outcompetes most weeds, but you will still need to do some weeding by hand to prevent rogue weed foliage from getting into your harvest.

## Harvest

Cut the leaves with scissors or a knife, leaving about 5 cm (2 inches) at the first cut to make sure you don't damage the growing tip. You can take the second cut a little lower. The seeds can be eaten green (and added to pasta dishes, bread, and stews) or left to ripen for the more usual, completely ripened, brown coriander seeds. The harvesting of coriander seeds is a perfect (and fragrant) volunteer job.

## Container Tips

Coriander grows well even in a small container, ideally in a cool location where temperature variations are relatively few. You can mix with other herbs, but always remember to keep the soil moist.

# Parsley

With a few different varieties to choose from, parsley is a great staple of many cuisines and is relatively easy to grow. Although it has a reputation for being difficult to germinate, I find that saving your own seeds and sowing it fresh makes a big difference.

**LIFESPAN**
Annual

**PLANT**
Sow directly outside when soil temperature is 10°C (50°F) or into seed flats six to eight weeks before last spring frost

**GROW IN**
Rich, well-drained soil

## Planting tips

Using good-quality fresh seeds is essential. Lightly cover the seeds on sowing, and give them up to 60 days at 16–18°C (61–64°F). If possible, just let any self-seeded plants survive wherever they spring up. Unlike its close relative coriander, which can get stressed if grown in seed flats, parsley will cope well, so consider sowing indoors in more controlled conditions and planting outside when ready. Sow again indoors in early summer for an autumn harvest if you live in a hot-summer area, and also in autumn for a winter crop.

## Cultivation

French and Italian flat-leaf parsley varieties are a little sensitive to cold conditions, but the curly type is hardy to frost. In harsh winters, you may need to protect overwintered plants with floating row covers. A sunny site is ideal, but the plants are tolerant of partial shade. Cut off the flower heads; they appear to extend the life of the crop.

## Weed Control

Parsley can be slow to germinate and grow initially, so weed well and keep a regular eye on seedlings as they germinate and develop.

## Harvest

For the flat-leaf varieties, treat like coriander and cut back the foliage to within about 5 cm (2 inches) of the base and then wait for regrowth. Curly parsley responds well if you restrict yourself to picking only the individual outer leaves; let the inner ones develop. This can be time-consuming if you are picking large quantities.

## Container Tips

Choose flat-leaf varieties for containers because they grow more quickly and are more tolerant of dry conditions. Water regularly so that the soil mix is kept just moist.

# Rosemary

Mediterranean in origin, rosemary can be thought
of almost as a winter plant in mild-winter areas,
because it does well as low as about -6.5°C (20°F).
The bushes also flower at the end of winter,
making them useful for attracting pollinating
insects to your community garden.

**LIFESPAN**
Short-lived perennial

**PLANT**
When nighttime temperatures
are above 13°C (55°F)

**GROW IN**
Any well-drained soil in sun

## Planting Tips

Water new plants in well for the first
couple of seasons. In windy sites,
provide some protection from the wind.

## Cultivation

Keep rosemary regularly trimmed, even
if you are not cutting for use, because
they have a tendency to sprawl and
get leggy. Avoid cutting into the older
hard wood, which is a temptation on
plants that have been allowed to get
big; the shrub may not recover. Taller
cultivars can reach more than 90 cm
(3 feet) and might need support.

## Weed Control

Help new plants get established by
removing weeds growing nearby.
On mature plants, a layer of fallen
leaves will collect around the plant;
these leaves release a chemical that
inhibits the germination of other seeds
around them. As a result, the ground
around rosemary plants tends to be
naturally weed free.

## Harvest

Cut 10–15 cm (4–6 inches) long sprigs
of new growth as needed, at any time
of the year. This also encourages new
growth from lower on the plant, so it is
good to do this regularly.

## Container Tips

Rosemary is well suited to container
growing. Try growing one of the
trailing (prostrate) varieties, which will
tumble beautifully over the edge of a
container. In areas with cold winters,
you can move the pot to a more
sheltered position to protect it.

# Thyme

The huge variety of thymes available, such as lemon thyme, vary slightly in growth habit. Mostly they are low, ground-hugging plants suitable for naturalizing in between gaps in paving or any other well-drained and sunny site. They are ornamental, particularly when they are in flower.

**LIFESPAN**
Short-lived perennial

**PLANT**
Sow seed or plant in spring or summer

**GROW IN**
Any light, well-drained soil in sun

## Planting Tips

Thyme is frost-hardy, and unless plants have become severely rootbound or their roots are sitting in water, it is hard to grow badly. If container-grown plants are a little leggy, replant them about 2.5 cm (1 inch) below ground level and cover the crown with soil. This will encourage the branches to root and will reinvigorate the plant.

## Cultivation

The main trick with thyme is pruning little and often to keep a constant supply of fresh young growth. For example, plant four plants and prune one every week in rotation; in this way, you will always have new foliage to use. For a good supply over winter, trim the plants in mid- to late summer and let them regrow without additional trimming.

## Weed Control

A good covering of thyme will help to prevent weed seeds from germinating, although, in the early stages, pull out any competing weeds by hand. Thyme will form a useful scented mat around the bottom of other plants, or at the edge of paths, where it will control weeds. In some situations, thyme can itself become a weed; in this case, you may need to trim the flowers off before it has a chance to seed.

## Harvest

If harvesting for chopping, take the youngest soft shoots, with or without the flowers. For harvesting as bouquet garni, you can take longer stems, including older wood.

## Container Tips

All varieties of thyme grow well in containers, although choosing spreading varieties that will trail over the sides will make better use of space. Try mixing with other herbs in the same container.

# Sage

Sage is one of the larger herbs, growing to about 60 cm (24 inches) tall if not clipped to size, so you won't need many plants. In mild climates, sage is one of those herbs that stays in leaf through winter, providing a useful source of antioxidants as well as having many uses in the kitchen.

**LIFESPAN**
Short-lived perennial

**PLANT**
Seedlings and potted plants in spring; rotted cuttings in summer

**GROW IN**
Any well-drained, sunny site

## Planting Tips

New plants establish more quickly once the soil has warmed up. Sage grows well from seeds, and whenever the beautiful blue flowers appear in summer, it is worth saving a few seeds. Sage doesn't like being dripped on, so avoid planting under trees or a building overhang.

## Cultivation

As with most of the woody herbs, trim little and often to keep the plants neat; a bushy and compact shape looks much nicer than a leggy plant, which will provide fewer fresh leaves and will be more prone to winter damage from winds and snow. It is not necessary to eat everything you cut. Leggy plants are also shorter-lived, although some growers routinely replace their bushes every four or five years to keep them productive and compact.

## Weed Control

Sage plants are vigorous, and weed control is not usually a problem once they are established. Creeping weeds can be a nuisance, so be sure that the ground is clean before planting.

## Harvest

Pick individual leaves and growing tips for kitchen use. Depending on your taste, they can be made into tea or chewed raw. Sprigs of 10 cm (4 inches) or longer can be cut for the vase; it is useful to cut low from time to time (even into the woody growth) because it encourages sprouting from farther down the bush.

## Container Tip

Sage does well in containers but needs to be pruned more often so that the plant remains neat and well clothed with foliage. Choose a less vigorous variety, such as variegated sage.

# Oregano

Perhaps one of the easiest herbs to grow, oregano is vigorous, spreading, and relatively frost-hardy. It is an essential ingredient for the perfect pizza; it can be eaten fresh or is perfect for drying. The plants have lovely summer flowers that are great for attracting wildlife.

**LIFESPAN**
Perennial

**PLANT**
Set young plants out in spring; plant divisions in autumn

**GROW IN**
Any well-drained, preferably fertile, sunny location

## Planting Tips

It is possible to sow oregano from seeds, but they are tiny, so just scatter the seeds onto fine seed-starting mix, water it in, and leave it uncovered. Mixing the seeds first with a little sand will produce a more even distribution. Alternatively, buy one plant and split it into smaller pieces as it grows to increase your stock.

## Cultivation

Trim back regularly to keep the plants bushy and to control their spread. Prune out dead stems when they are seen and old flower heads after flowering. Oregano keeps its leaves in milder climates, but for a reliable winter supply, shelter plants in a well-lit, frost-free location.

## Weed Control

Oregano spreads fast and can quickly cover ground, which makes it perfect for growing around trees or larger shrubs. It will outcompete most weeds.

## Harvest

Although you can harvest for most of the spring and summer, the flavour is best just before flowering, so pick in midsummer for drying. For fresh use, pick the soft shoots when they are about 2.5 cm (1 inch) or so long. For drying, cut the stems right back to just above the old growth to get the maximum harvest.

## Container Tips

Oregano works wonderfully in containers, trailing and tumbling over the edge. However, it forms a dense mat, so it is difficult to top up with fresh soil mix. Instead, repot and divide the plants every couple of years to keep them fresh. Growing it in a container is also a good way to stop it spreading among other plants.

# French Tarragon

French tarragon is a slightly difficult plant because it won't grow from seeds and is neither hardy nor vigorous. With a distinctive and delicious flavour, its popularity with chefs makes it a handy plant to grow for community gardens looking for a little income.

**LIFESPAN**
Short-lived perennial

**PLANT**
Set plants in when dormant in autumn or spring

**GROW IN**
Fertile, well-drained, sandy soil in sun or partial shade

## Planting Tips

Because French tarragon produces sterile seeds, you will need to buy either plants or raise from cuttings in summer. Once you have a few plants, it is easy to divide the roots in early spring. Choose a sheltered site and make sure you have removed all perennial weeds from the ground before planting.

## Cultivation

French tarragon grows slowly, so if growing for all your members or even semi-commercially, you will need a few plants. Unlike many herbs, it does not spread uncontrollably and can be successfully interplanted with vegetable crops. The plants will survive a light frost, but in colder climates they need to be either sheltered in a frost-free place or protected with a thick mulch over winter.

## Weed Control

With its delicate leaf and upright habit, French tarragon will need regular weeding by hand.

## Harvest

Do not cut all the foliage at one time because the plants can be a little slow to regrow. Instead, cut no more than one-third of the growth for each harvest and then let it regrow. It is a herb with a strong flavour, so you don't need a lot to give your cooking flavour.

## Container Tip

French tarragon grows well in a container. This will also make it easier to bring it in over winter, where it can be protected from frost.

# Mint

Many growers are suspicious of mint because it has a reputation for being invasive. With advanced planning, however, its roots can easily be confined and you will soon find it a useful addition to a community garden, especially for fresh tea when your members need revitalizing.

**LIFESPAN**
Perennial

**PLANT**
Sow seeds in spring, plant divisions in autumn, or buy a potted variety for planting anytime

**GROW IN**
Most soil in sun or partial shade

## Planting Tips

Mint is so tough and vibrant that you can plant it pretty much anytime of year, and as long as it gets some water, it will survive. The seeds are also easy to grow, but tiny, so just sprinkle them onto the surface of some seed-starting mix and water gently—there is no need to cover the seeds. The main problem is controlling mint, so consider growing it in a separate bed or sinking a big container into the soil. Because there are so many different types of mint to try, with unique flavours, such as chocolate mint or spearmint, you may find yourself planting several containers of various types.

## Cultivation

You'll have to work hard to kill mint, but occasionally the middle of a clump will die off. In such cases, dig out the dead section and replant with a piece that is taken from another, more vigorous, section.

## Weed Control

The only weed is the mint itself, so do not plant it where its spreading roots will cause problems. Keep it confined and well away from other, less competitive, crops.

## Harvest

Pick regularly to keep the tips fresh as soon as the shoots appear in spring. For dried mint, cut just before flowering in early summer. For community gardens wanting an income, mint tips can be sold to chefs wanting to decorate their dessert plates.

## Container Tips

Mint is ideally suited for container growing because this stops it from invading your garden. Keep it watered regularly—mint does not like arid conditions—and choose one of the less vigorous varieties to avoid it getting rootbound too quickly. Divide and repot every two or three years.

# Picture Credits

# Glossary

**ABSCISIC ACID** A plant hormone that plays an important role in plant development, including dormancy.

**ACHENE** A dry one-seeded fruit, which does not open to release the seed.

**ADVENTITIOUS ROOT** Root that arises from the stem and not from another root.

**ALTERNATE** Each leaf grows alternately one at a time along the stem.

**ANNUAL** Life cycle lasts one season.

**ARABLE** Land capable of being cultivated.

**AXIL** Where the leaf joins the stem.

**BIENNIAL** Completes life cycle in two seasons, germinating and growing the first season and flowering and setting seed in the second.

**BIODIVERSITY** The variety of life in the world.

**BIOTECHNOLOGY** Manufacturing or technological engineering that uses living organisms.

**BIPINNATIFID** Pinnate leaves with doubly cut segments.

**BOLTING** Usually referring to vegetables when they send up a flower stalk too quickly. This means the plant has gone to seed early and often results in a much lower yield.

**BRACT** A modified leaf protecting the flower.

**BROADCAST SEEDS** The method of casting seeds over a broad area, onto pre-prepared ground.

**BULB** An underground modified bud and stem used as a food storage organ by dormant plants.

**CALCAREOUS** Lime-rich.

**CHLOROPHYLL** Green photosynthetic pigment responsible for trapping radiant light.

**CHLOROPLAST** The portion of a plant cell that contains chlorophyll.

**CLOCHE** A protective cover for outdoor plants.

**COLD FRAME** An unheated frame with a glass or plastic top where small plants and seedlings are hardened off.

**COMPOUND** A flower made up of numerous florets.

**CROSS BREEDING** The mating of two distinctly different varieties or species of plants to produce a hybrid, or cross breed. Cross breeding can occur naturally, or artificially by human intervention.

**CROSS-POLLINATE** The transfer of pollen between two different plants.

**CRYOPRESERVATION** The preservation of living organisms by cooling them to extremely low temperatures.

**CUT-AND-COME-AGAIN** Describes edible leafy plants where the leaves are cut while the plant is still growing in the ground. The leaves then re-grow (come again).

**CYME** Flat-topped cluster of flowers.

**DAMPING OFF** A lifethreatening disease of seedlings caused by a variety of fungi.

**DEADHEADING** The removal of dead or spent flowers from a plant. Deadheading prevents the formation of seed heads.

**DIFFUSION** The movement of a substance from an area of higher concentration to an area of lower concentration until a balance is reached.

**DIOECIOUS** Male and female reproductive organs found on separate plants.

**DISC FLORET** Small tubular petal-like flower at the centre of the flower head.

**ECOSYSTEM** The complete biological activity and interaction of a community of organisms within an area.

**ENVIRONMENTALIST** Someone who works toward protecting and improving the natural environment

**ENZYMES** Complex chemicals produced by plant cells, which help activate processes such as photosynthesis.

**EPIPHYTIC** A plant that grows on another for support.

**ETHNOBOTANY** The study of plants and their relationships with human society.

**EVERGREEN** A plant that retains its leaves all year round.

**FILIAL GENERATION** A generation of offspring produced from cross breeding genetically different plants. The first generation is referred to as the F1 generation, followed by the F2 generation, and so on.

**FLORET** Tiny flower.

**GENETIC DRIFT** The change in the genetic variety of a population over time due to the random passing on of genes from one population to the next. This usually only affects smaller populations, as the diversity weakens over time.

**GERMINATION** Transition of seed to seedling.

**GLABROUS** Smooth, lacking hairs or bristles.

**HABIT** The general appearance of a plant; for example, spreading, upright, bushy or creeping.

**HERBACEOUS** Non-woody plants whose leaves and stems die down at the end of the growing season.

**HERBARIUM** A collection of preserved plant specimens.

**HERBICIDE** A chemical or organic-based agent used to kill unwanted plants.

**HERMAPHRODITE** Male and female organs found on the same flower.

**HETEROPHYLLY** Plants that have leaves of different shapes on the same plant.

**INDIGENOUS** Native to a particular region.

**INSECTICIDE** Chemical or organic-based agent used to control damaging insects.

**INTERBREEDING** When two genetically similar plants mate.

**IN-VITRO** An experimental process performed outside a living organism in an artificial environment such as a test tube.

**INVOLUCRE** A protective whorl of bracts surrounding a flower.

**LEPIDOPTERA** Moths and butterflies.

**LIQUID NITROGEN** Nitrogen in liquid form, used for freezing.

**LOBED** Deeply indented leaves.

**MERICARP** A single, separating part of a manyseeded dry fruit.

**MIDRIB** A strong central leaf vein.

**MONOECIOUS** Male and female reproductive organs found on the same plant.

**NODE** A point on the stem where the leaves emerge.

**NODULE** An outgrowth from the roots of legumes containing nitrogen-fixing bacteria.

**OBLANCEOLATE** Lanceshaped but with the widest part at the tip of the leaf and the narrowest at the base.

**OBLONG** A leaf with a length greater than the width.

**ORBICULAR** Circular.

**OBLONGOID** An elongated circle.

**ORGANISM** An independent living thing.

**PANICLE** Branched compound flower of racemes arranged around the main floral stem.

**PAPPUS** A covering of scales; feathery hairs or bristles at the apex of the seed.

**PARASITIC WASP** Wasp that feeds on pest insects.

**PATENT LAWS** A written law concerned with ownership rights.

**PERENNIAL** A plant that lasts for more than two growing seasons.

**PESTICIDE** A chemical substance used to kill pests, especially insects.

**PH** A measure of the acidity or

alkalinity of a soil or solution, on a scale of 0 to 14, where 7 is neutral. A value above 7 is alkaline, and a value below 7 is acidic.

**PINNATE** A leaf made of leaflets arranged in a row on either side of the midrib.

**PINNATIPARTITE** A leaf with incisioned lobes extending over halfway toward the midrib.

**RACEME** A cluster of tightly packed flowers growing in long thin columns (e.g. foxglove); the flowers at the base open first.

**RAY FLORET** The petal-like outer floret of a flower head (e.g. sunflower).

**RECEPTACLE** Swollen area at the stem tip where the flower grows.

**REFLEXED** Bent downwards and turned backwards.

**REPOPULATE** To introduce a number of species into an area especially with the aim to rebuild or sustain a population.

**RHIZOME** An underground horizontal stem that sends out roots and shoots.

**ROOT BALL** The clump of roots of a container-grown plant, consisting of the roots and soil.

**ROSETTE** A low-growing circular arrangement of leaves.

**RUNNER** Horizontal stem sent out from the base of a plant, which produces new plants from buds along the stem and at the tips.

**SCARIFICATION** Cutting the seed coat to encourage germination by allowing water to penetrate the seed.

**SEED DRILL** A shallow trench into which seeds are sown.

**SEED SOVEREIGNTY** Power over seed supply. This has moved progressively from farmers to seed companies since the 1930s.

**SELF-FERTILE** Capable of self-fertilization without the need for another plant.

**SELF-POLLINATE** The fertilization of a flower by its own pollen, from its anthers to its stigma.

**SELF-SEED** A plant naturally regenerated from seed without human intervention.

**SEPALS** Modified leaves that occur outside the petals and protect the flower bud.

**SILIQUA** A long dry seed capsule with a central partition to which the seeds are attached.

**STRATIFICATION** Pretreating seeds to help germination by simulating natural winter conditions, e.g. freezing.

**SOIL TYPE** Classification of soil based on its sand, silt, clay and organic matter content and pH.

**SPATULATE** Broad and rounded at the top with a narrow base.

**SPURRED** A spiked part of a flower.

**SUBSHRUB** A low-growing woody perennial.

**SUBSOIL** The soil between topsoil and bedrock.

**TERMINATOR TECHNOLOGY** The use of genetic technology to create plants that produce sterile seeds, which are incapable of producing further offspring.

**TRANSITION TOWN INITIATIVE** A community-led process that helps a village, town or city become stronger through initiatives to improve areas such as food transport and energy.

**TRIFOLIATE** A leaf divided into three leaflets.

**TRIPINNATE** A leaf divided three times, as in ferns.

**TRUE SEEDS** Those that retain the distinguishing characteristics of their parents.

**UMBEL** A multiplestemmed umbrellashaped cluster of flowers.

**UMBELLIFEROUS** Plants belonging to the *Umbelliferae* family, or plants that produce umbels, i.e. flat-topped flower heads composed of many short stalks originating from the tip of a central stem.

**WHORL** Arrangement of leaves, petals, etc. in a circular or spiral pattern.

**VEGETATIVE PROPAGATION** Asexual reproduction of plants through cuttings, division, runners.

**VIABLE** (of seeds) Able to germinate.

# Index

# About the Author

**Ben Raskin** is the Head of Horticulture and Agroforestry at the Soil Association in the UK, and author of *Zero-Waste Gardening* (2021). He also manages a pioneering agroforestry planting on a 600-hectare (1,480-acre) farm in the South West of England. Ben got the gardening bug while working on an organic vineyard in northern Italy, and has worked in horticulture for thirty years, including a stint as Assistant Head Gardener at the UK charity Garden Organic. He also wrote *Plant a Tree and Retree the World, Compost; Grow;* and *Bees, Bugs & Butterflies* all published by Leaping Hare Press.

**The Soil Association** is the charity that joins forces with nature for a better future, a world with good health, in balance with nature and a safe climate. Working with everyone to transform the way we eat, farm and care for our natural world, we build real solutions from the ground up. Together, we are a force for nature. soilassociation.org

# Acknowledgements

Thanks to all my friends at the The Community Farm and especially Dave for his advice on the legal chapter and Andy and Alison for dedication beyond the call of duty. Thanks also to the CSA Network UK and Soil Association colleagues past and present for their inspiration and guidance. Thanks to Ruth for forgiving me the lost evenings and weekends, and everything else.

*Leaping Hare Press*

First published in 2017.
This edition published in 2024 by Leaping Hare Press,
an imprint of The Quarto Group.
One Triptych Place,
London, SE1 9SH
United Kingdom
T (0)20 7700 6700
www.Quarto.com

A catalogue record for this book is available from the British Library.

ISBN 978-0-7112-8736-5
Ebook ISBN 978-0-7112-8737-2

Senior commissioning editor: Monica Perdoni
Designer: Sally Bond
Junior Designer: Daisy Woods
Editorial director: Jennifer Barr
Editorial assistant: Nayima Ali
Production: Maeve Healy
Illustrations: Thomas Pullin

10 9 8 7 6 5 4 3 2

Printed in China

*The information provided in this book is for informational purposes only and is intended to offer guidance on seed saving and swapping practices. The author encourages readers to exercise caution by verifying that crops will not crossbreed with wild or poisonous relatives, which may result in potentially toxic offspring. Any use of the information contained within this book is at the reader's own discretion and risk.*

*The author, contributors and publisher make no representations or warranties with respect to the accuracy, completeness or suitability for a particular purpose of the content of this book. To the fullest extent permitted by law, they disclaim all liability for any errors, omissions, or inaccuracies, as well as for any injury, loss, damage, or expense that may arise from the use or misuse of the information provided.*

*Readers are advised to consult a qualified expert before undertaking any gardening or seed-saving activities to ensure safe and responsible practices.*